CHRIST AND CONSCIOUSNESS

CHRIST AND CONSCIOUSNESS

Exploring Christ's Contribution to Human Consciousness

The Origins and Development of
Christian Consciousness

WILLIAM M. THOMPSON

PAULIST PRESS
New York/Ramsey/Toronto

Library of Congress
Catalog Card Number: 77-83557

ISBN: 0-8091-2066-6

Published by Paulist Press
Editorial Office: 1865 Broadway, New York, N.Y. 10023
Business Office: 545 Island Road, Ramsey, N.J. 07446

Printed and bound in the
United States of America

Contents

PART IV

SOME FURTHER PROBINGS

TO
PATRICIA MARIE
Intuitive Theologian

———

My Guide Along The Way

Foreword

This book is largely the result of my own development in consciousness. And as that development is never an isolated one, but largely the result of the friends I've been blessed with, the friendly "adversaries" I've been challenged by, the works I've been provoked by, and the living masters I've been stimulated by, a great amount of thanks is first in order. I am learning more and more that the depth of one's thankfulness is largely a measure of his development.

Those who should receive thanks must largely remain nameless, though their not being named is no measure of my deep thanks to them. I must first mention, though, my wife Pat, a very helpful theologian in her own way, who put up with the many compulsions and anxieties that "show their head" in writing a book like this, and was deeply altruistic enough to both sustain me throughout and oftentimes challenge me. Second, I must thank my very good friends Peter Chirico and Gregory Baum. The former inspired me to choose theology for my ministry; the latter greatly deepened that initial inspiration. The continued friendship and stimulating conversations with both have greatly nurtured whatever theological insight I possess. Third, the many conversations with the faculty members of St. Mary's Seminary and University, Baltimore, St. Patrick's Seminary, Menlo Park, Carroll College, Helena, and St. Michael's College of the University of Toronto have led me on the path which at this stage of my journey has culminated in this book. Finally, I deeply thank Carolyn Kobielus who somewhat miraculously transformed my script into a legible and typed manuscript.

In the end, however, I must take responsibility for whatever misguidance results from the reading of this book.

PART I
THEOLOGY
AND
HUMAN CONSCIOUSNESS

I
Theology and Studies on the Development of Human Consciousness

Books on "consciousness" abound today, and all of them, in one way or another, seem to be motivated by a number of basic convictions. For one thing, the quality of consciousness we have seems to determine our approach to life and the various options we seem to have open to us within this life. We may be very "rationalistically" oriented, and then our life becomes the solution to a syllogism. We would then strive for order and neatness, for logic in all we do. Life may have some unanswered questions, but our rational mind will eventually solve them. Our stomach for the mysterious and the aweful is something we temporarily put up with. Today, most books seem to notice this rationalistic trend and some of its restrictive consequences, and so we come to another of their convictions: Is there not something dreadfully wrong with human consciousness? Have we perhaps needlessly restricted its range of possibilities? Can we not perhaps widen it somewhat? Although some of these books may be needlessly prejudicial and over-reactive to the rationalistic trend in human consciousness mentioned above, most seem rightly concerned to restore to human consciousness its wholeness. But what has seemed lacking so far is any specific Christian theological attempt to show how Christianity has shared and can further share in this authentic aspiration to restore to human consciousness its wholeness. This book would like to make some small contribution to this task.

It was Karl Jaspers' *The Origin and Goal of History* that first suggested to me the possibility of this study. In that masterful work he spoke of three great transitions in the history of humanity: (1) the axial transition of the first millennium when genuine personal consciousness as we know it today emerged; (2) our present rationalistic and technological age, which both

5

threatens the destruction of the axial breakthrough by restricting human consciousness to only one of its capacities and simultaneously promises a heightened awareness of human personhood; (3) the future planetization of humanity, which both promises a further expansion of human consciousness beyond cultural boundaries and demands it, for as the world becomes increasingly one, what happens now becomes absolutely decisive: "There is no longer anything outside it."[1] My thesis, suggested by Jaspers, is a simple one: Christians, too, participate in these three great historical transitions, and the task I have set myself is to explore how Christians have entered and can enter into them, and what happens to Christianity as a result of this.

A number of basic assumptions inform this study. First, I place great stress on the notion of human "consciousness," for I am convinced that it is man's consciousness itself that determines what man can imagine as a genuine possibility. This need not nor should it be understood in a subjectivist or idealist fashion, as if every human possibility that has ever been conceived were simply the creation of man's mind. Were that the case, such human beliefs as man's radical individuality and personhood and religious beliefs such as man's eternal destiny and trust in a transcendent mystery would be seriously jeopardized. But my analysis will be historical and phenomenological, rather than metaphysical. Though I will make some observations on the truth-status of what man has conceived, I am more properly concerned with how man has come to imagine certain possibilities, and that leads us to some such notion as human "consciousness." Why and how did notions such as human personhood, freedom, love, God, eternal life, the "Kingdom" of Christ, the resurrection, salvation, etc., arise? What enabled man to imagine these possibilities? Do our earliest records indicate that man always imagined these possibilities in the same way? If not, does this not argue for some kind of development in man's consciousness itself?

I am using "consciousness" then, in its widest meaning, as referring to any kind of "awareness" the person possesses. Its existence cannot be empirically proven, for it is not an object present to the senses like a tree or a chair. With these latter objects, one can employ the ordinary criteria of correspondence to verify their existence: Does my perception of them correspond to the actual object? One must take a more indirect route to arrive at the notion of consciousness: it is implied as the condition of the possibility of my ever being aware of the need to verify a chair's existence. Because it is not directly perceivable, we normally do not advert to its existence, and one of the goals of this essay is to sensitize ourselves to its extraordinary importance for the quality of our lives.

By equating consciousness with awareness, we can easily understand that the notion refers to a continuum that embraces the wide variety of modes of human awareness. The child's awareness differs from the adult's, for the latter's experience has greatly expanded the range of possibilities that he can imagine. The child's awareness in sleep greatly differs from his awareness while awake. Consciousness, then, is a heuristic notion to describe modes of awareness, and this is the fundamental insight governing psychoanalysis and its differentiation of consciousness into subconscious, conscious, and unconscious.[2] This insight enables us to understand that one's consciousness shifts, expands, restricts, and develops, and this essay will simply seek to explore some of the fundamental ways in which this has occurred in man's history.

I think we can go further, too, and speak of fundamental modes of awareness. It was Freud who greatly sensitized us to the insight that a particular mode of awareness generally governs the human psyche, and all other modes are "controlled" or filtered by it. Thus he spoke of the "unconscious" as controlling the behavior of his patients. Without adhering to the Freudian categories, I think it important to appropriate his insight that there are dominant or fundamental modes of awareness governing our psyches and behavior. We can test this for ourselves by alluding to the fact that while we engage from time to time in fantasy, nonetheless it is our more rational and self-critical awareness that governs our behavior. We can extrapolate from the Freudian insight about a governing mode of consciousness and speculate whether different epochs have fos-

tered differing governing modes. This study will also explore
this possibility, especially as it relates to the development of
Christian consciousness.

My second assumption is that, as man's consciousness
complexifies, so too does his corresponding ability to imagine
human possibilities. This second assumption, I think it safe to
say, enjoys a great amount of support from theoretical psychologists and cultural analysts. On the psychological level the
studies of Jean Piaget[3] have done much to forward this thesis.
In his own analysis of the moral reasoning of children, he has
described a process in which children progress from "heteronomy" to "autonomy." The crucial factor here is the increasing complexification of the child. Because the child in the
earliest stages does not yet know his own identity as an autonomous individual, he finds it in submission to the rules imposed on him by adults (thus "heteronomy"). As the child's experience complexifies, primarily through social intercourse and
the experience of mutual respect, he becomes aware of himself
as autonomous. This new-found awareness broadens the manner in which he understands himself. It also expands the range
of possibilities of what he can imagine: his life need no longer
be based on submission to adult rules but can be one in which
he strives for his own individual fulfillment.

The basic insight into the linkage between complexification and consciousness has been further explored by the Har-
vard psychologist Lawrence Kohlberg.[4] By concentrating on
the full range of human development, thus including adults, he
has contributed a wider perspective on how human consciousness expands. His goal is to analyze possible patterns in the
processes by which humans achieve autonomous individuation,
and his governing assumption is that an increasing development in consciousness is facilitated through an increasing complexification of experience. Since I will rely on Kohlberg later
in this study, I will reserve my discussion of his findings until
then. But I would like to indicate why I have found his findings
attractive, and why I have preferred his theory of human development to the many others advanced by psychologists. Basically Kohlberg attempts to steer a middle course between the assumption that all behavior is innate and psychically determined

from one's earliest childhood and that which would hold that it is ultimately a function of social conditioning. Neither view has won a wide consensus, and Kohlberg, by concentrating on the cognitive aspects of development, has been able to formulate a view which does justice to both alternatives and yet goes beyond them. The innate factor, if you will, is the cognitive capacity to develop one's consciousness, but this consciousness can only develop through the complexification afforded by one's social conditioning.

Our linkage between complexification and consciousness has been further explored on the cultural level. That is, just as the individual's consciousness develops through an increasing complexification of his experience, so too the historical evidence enables us to extrapolate from this and to postulate that the race as a whole—in representative figures—has developed its consciousness as its experience has complexified. Thanks to the work of Lewis Mumford, Erich Neumann, John Dunne, Herbert Richardson, and Eric Voegelin,[5] this thesis seems to enjoy a good amount of support also. Basically what has been noted is that the race as a whole has undergone a development, from the basically undifferentiated experience and consciousness of earliest man to the increasingly differentiated experience and consciousness of modern man. The importance of this insight is that it provides us with a framework from which to understand Jaspers' thesis about the great historical transitions that man has undergone. Each transition in history can be understood—in the ideal—as a new complexification of human experience which fosters a corresponding development in man's consciousness. Thus, we could speak of three great epochs in human consciousness: (1) axial consciousness, in which human personhood emerged; (2) our modern consciousness, in which science and technology emerged; (3) the future planetary consciousness, whose implications are not yet clear. Jaspers' thesis is, of course, that these transitions in consciousness are so fundamental that they govern the very way man conceives of himself. With each new transition man has discovered new possibilities for himself, but so too have the threats to human development increased. The point of this book is, of course, to analyze these developments in human consciousness which seem fostered and called for by each of these epochs, and to explore their implications for Christianity.

My third assumption is that man's complexification in experience and corresponding differentiation in consciousness provides us with a heuristic for understanding both the emergence and the possible developments in Christian consciousness itself. For example, what complexification in experience and corresponding consciousness underlies the emergence of Christianity? What new human possibilities could man imagine as a result of that? What further developments might Christians be expected to undergo as they enter into and appropriate the discoveries of both our modern technological age and our projected future planetary one? Under the influence of Jaspers, I will try to maintain that Christianity is a fully axial phenomenon, and indeed radicalizes the axial discovery of human personhood. I will then further explore the challenges posed for Christianity by Jaspers' modern and planetary epochs, attempting to show that Christianity can fully appropriate their discoveries and even contribute to them. Our ultimate aim is to provide a tentative theory of the origins and development of Christian consciousness itself.[6]

Why have I decided to attempt this study? Three reasons have brought me to it. First, it seems a safe assumption that each individual "re-enacts" the developments in consciousness of the race as a whole. As the race has, at least in principle, moved from the undifferentiated world of primitive man to the sophisticated and increasingly differentiated one of modern man, so the individual must undergo a similar development. Each epoch of human development demands new skills and new abilities in understanding, and if the individual is to harmoniously live as a participant in his own epoch, he will have to undergo the required development. After all, we can go through life in two ways, according to Jung: "One is to walk through upright and the other is to be dragged through."[7] If the first alternative is chosen, man has no choice but that of undergoing the development called for by his epoch. If this applies to humanity in general, it applies to Christianity in particular. Not a few of the difficulties in the Church today stem from a refusal to undergo the development demanded by our

times. For example, if Christianity is basically an axial phenomenon which radicalizes the axial discovery of human personhood and autonomy, what are we to make of those church-
men who would lead us to believe that Christianity has nothing
to do with human fulfillment? What are we to make of those
Church structures which do not foster an authentic sense of
human personhood and autonomy? As the world becomes increasingly sophisticated scientifically and historically in our
modern epoch, how will the Church be able to give an account
of itself to modern man if it speaks only the language of pre-
moderns? And finally, if Jaspers is correct about the emergence
of a planetary epoch, will this not demand of Christianity a
new self-understanding, enabling it happily to overcome its im-
perialistic tendencies and to learn from the valid experiences
and insights of others?

My second reason has to do with the growing breakdown
of the cultural phenomenon known as "Christendom." This
latter is a technical term referring to the epoch when Christianity was the predominant cultural form of religion in the
West. This is still the case in certain isolated countries in which
Roman Catholicism or Protestantism exists as the only legally
recognized state religion. What we are noticing increasingly
today with the secularization of the West is the breakdown of
Christendom's cultural dominance. Now this fact needs to be
carefully greeted by the contemporary Christian. On the one
hand it can lead to a deepening of Christianity in which religionists learn to clearly distinguish outmoded cultural forms of
Christendom from the core of Christian belief. On the other
hand, it raises new difficulties. For when the culture fostered a
"religious" atmosphere, individuals could culturally assimilate
Christianity much as they would assimilate other cultural customs. This is increasingly no longer the case, and we must expect that Christians will increasingly only be and remain such
if they can grasp the real relevance to their lives of the Christian faith. Thus the basic need to clarify the real contribution
that Christianity can make to human development and human
consciousness.

My final reason is that of our growing awareness of the
phenomenon of pluralism. What has made this a heightened

problem in our own times is our quite radical sense of human historicity and our increasing planetary experience of the world. The awareness of human historicity sensitizes us to the cultural conditioning underlying all forms of belief and thought systems. While the West knew a certain form of pluralism formerly—Scotists and Thomists, Catholics and Protestants, Muslims and Spanish Catholics, etc.—it was a pluralism within a commonly accepted framework of beliefs. Catholics and Protestants disagreed on the papacy, but they *both* shared a belief in God. Today it is the very framework that is under question and known to be historically conditioned. Our contemporary planetary experience further radicalizes the awareness of pluralism by confronting the contemporary Christian, primarily through the communications media, with radically opposing views of the human quest.[8]

One manner of handling pluralism is what I would call "conceptual." Since pluralism heightens the sense of the opposition between differing conceptual schemes of reality, one tries to devise an over-reaching conceptual apparatus accounting for all the difficulties. But this only heightens the problem, for how does one adjudicate the relative merits of dialectical materialism as opposed to Christianity? They each start from differing presuppositions about the nature of reality and their concepts carry different meanings. Furthermore, this approach presupposes that there is a perfect conceptual scheme which man can devise. But it is precisely this presupposition which is under question in our pluralistic age. This point has been well made by Stephen Toulmin:

> We must set aside the traditional cult of systematicity, and carry our analysis of concepts—in science and elsewhere— back to its proper starting point. The intellectual content of any rational activity forms neither a single logical system, nor a temporal sequence of such systems. Rather, it is an *intellectual enterprise* whose "rationality" lies in the procedures governing its historical development and evolution.[9]

Toulmin's proposal for pluralism—and I share it with him —is not some "perfect" conceptual scheme, but a *heightened consciousness* aware of its own developing ability to rationalize, criticize, and evaluate. Toulmin could be said to be "heightening" or illuminating the consciousness of his readers. I have learned much from Toulmin and would like to think that this study is a similar exercise in consciousness-heightening. I clearly am not proposing a new conceptual view of what Christianity is. Rather what I am attempting is to aid the Christian in appropriating and developing his own Christian consciousness. To that extent his own Christian ability to evaluate and discern will provide him with a means for coping with pluralism—indeed for welcoming it as well as critiquing it.

As one reads the text, he will notice my heavy dependence upon certain authors. The influence of Karl Jaspers upon me has been profound, and this book is simply a Christian exploration of his masterful *The Origin and Goal of History*. Both John Dunne and Herbert Richardson have attempted analyses in specific fields which also reflect the influence of Jaspers. I have relied upon them and learned much from them, but hopefully my focus is sufficiently different to justify this book. For while each of these authors proposes and develops a theory of the development of human consciousness, none specifically takes up the Christian "form" of that development. It was Eric Voegelin who first alerted me to the possibility of qualitative modifications in human consciousness stemming from the different participants of the axial period. I have learned from this clue and try to propose that while Christianity is a partner in the one axial period, it has its own qualitative contributions to make. The excellent work of John Cobb, *The Structure of Christian Existence*, further encouraged me in this proposal. He specifically takes up the question of the Christian contribution to the axial period, and my own study has been decisively altered in its structure as a result of studying Cobb. However, a number of significant differences exist. First, Cobb relies upon Erich Neumann and employs a modified Jungian approach to human consciousness. I have preferred Piaget and Kohlberg, and thus avoid the notion of the "unconscious." Second, he most fully and masterfully explores the Christian experience of the spirit and understands this as the qualitative contribution of Christianity to the axial period. Our conclusions are similar, but I have concentrated on the resurrection belief as the key factor, which in turn illuminates the Christian experience of the spirit. Cobb alludes to the resurrection appearances, and his doing so fortified me in my own resolve, but I felt a more complete explanation of the resurrection belief was called for. Finally, Cobb does not take up the later possible developments in Christian consciousness stemming from Jaspers' modern and planetary epochs. I felt that our times call for this, and so I have pushed my analysis beyond the axial period.

Further, throughout this book a number of metaphysical questions will recur from time to time. Most prominently, of course, the truth-status of the Hebraic discovery of a transcendent God and the Christian belief in the risen Christ will appear problematic. Basically, I only want to point out that my focus is primarily "meaning" rather than "truth," to employ the distinction of the linguistic analysts. One must first know what it is one is seeking to establish before entering into the realm of metaphysics. For example, as my analysis will show, the Hebraic discovery of a transcendent God refers to a strictly transcendent reality, and not to a "particular being" within the world. Metaphysically this would mean that one could not verify this "being's" existence through the ordinary criteria of correspondence widely employed in philosophy. One simply cannot check one's "idea" of God against some empirical object in the world to seek for correspondence. The metaphysician, then, precisely because he knows the "meaning" of what he seeks to establish, will have to alter his canons of verifiability accordingly. If there are no direct, empirical checks on the idea of God, then an "indirect" route seems called for. Gordon Kaufman has perhaps most clearly noted this, and I could do no better than to recommend his various proposals to the metaphysician.[10] As he puts it with reference to the idea of "God": "The most a theologian can do is attempt to show that the interpretation of the facts of experience and life, which he or she has set forth, holds within it greater likelihood than any other for opening up the future into which humankind is moving—making available new possibilities, raising new hopes, enabling men and women to move to new levels of humanness and humaneness, instead of closing off options and restricting or inhibiting growth into a fuller humanity."[11] Our analysis needs to be complemented by a more properly metaphysical one, but hopefully this lays a kind of groundwork for that later task. For any metaphysical scheme will always be a further extrapolation from the level of consciousness that one has attained. Put traditionally, this means that a metaphysical exploration of Christ (Christology) will always be the result of soteriology (the awareness of Christ in the Christian consciousness itself).

Finally, I have felt it necessary and helpful to offer observations on what I call the "Oriental axis," meaning by this primarily Buddhism, but also indirectly Taoism and Hinduism. Necessary, because the Orient, too, was an authentic participant in the axial period. Helpful, because it offers us a clarification of Christianity by contrast. First, however, my observations are highly tentative and subject to correction from Oriental scholars more conversant with the field. Second, Oriental studies, while now undergoing a great renewal, are in a state of flux, and it is difficult to make the kinds of generalizations possible in Christian studies. Third, the one element that seems to enjoy a basic consensus in matters Oriental is the Oriental attempt to "relativize" the axial awareness of individuation through altered states of consciousness. Thus, it is only this facet of the matter that I have explored in this book. It is an important one, for I think it delimits the specifically Oriental contribution to the axial period, and perhaps can go far in explaining why the Western emphasis on rationality did not develop in the Orient. Furthermore, I in no way intend to imply that because the Western trend toward rationality did not occur in the East, therefore the East is "inferior." Indeed, the current Western interest in altered states of consciousness (more intuitive and less rationalistic) would seem to indicate that the Orient made a discovery of enduring importance for human development. But what seems puzzling to me is why the Oriental axis went in only this one direction (altered states of consciousness), while Judaeo-Christianity went in two directions, both the more rational one as well as the Oriental one in its mystical trend. This singularity of the Orient, I hope, justifies my exclusive concentration on this one aspect of its multifaceted reality.

Notes

1. Karl Jaspers, *The Origin and Goal of History* (New Haven, 1953), p. 140.

2. I have not employed the Freudian classification. Even the Freudian school employs "unconscious" and "subconscious" as heuristic terms, referring to what is at least latent in consciousness. "Consciousness" is clearly the governing term.

3. Cf. Jean Piaget, *The Moral Judgment of the Child* (New York, 1965), and *Science of Education and the Psychology of the Child* (New York, 1971); and D. MacRee, "A Test of Piaget's Theories of Moral Development," *Journal of Abnormal and Social Psychology* 49 (1954) 14-18.

4. Relevant bibliographies are found in Ronald Duska and Mariellen Whelan, *Moral Development: A Guide to Piaget and Kohlberg* (New York, 1975), and Brian P. Hall, *The Development of Consciousness* (New York, 1976).

5. Cf. Lewis Mumford, *The Transformations of Man* (New York, 1956); Erich Neumann, *The Origins and History of Consciousness* (New Haven, 1954); John Dunne, *The Way of All the Earth* (New York, 1972); Herbert W. Richardson, *Nun, Witch, Playmate: The Americanization of Sex* (New York, 1971); and Eric Voegelin, *Order and History* (Louisiana, 1956-1974), 4 vols.

6. The objections to such an approach to the Christian phenomenon will be explored in Chapters 2 and 3.

7. John Dunne, *ibid.,* p. 151, relying on Carl Jung, *Answer to Job* (New York, 1960), p. 185.

8. For a more detailed analysis, with references, see my "Rahner's Theology of Pluralism," *The Ecumenist* 11 (1973) 17-22.

9. See Stephen Toulmin, *Human Understanding,* Vol. I (Princeton, 1972), for a masterful critique of conceptualism. Cf. especially p. 85 for this citation, and also p. 84; "The first step is to reject the commitment to logical systematicity which makes absolutism and relativism appear the only alternatives available. This decision brings us to the heart of the matter. For it was, in fact, always a mistake to identify rationality and logicality—to suppose, that is, that the rational ambitions of any historically developing intellectual activity can be understood entirely in terms of the propositional or conceptual systems in which its intellectual content may be expressed at one or another time. Questions of 'rationality' are concerned, precisely, not with the particular intellectual doctrines that a man—or professional group—adopts at any given time, but rather with *the conditions on which, and the manner in which, he is prepared to criticize and change those doctrines as time goes on.*"

10. Cf. Gordon D. Kaufman, *God the Problem* (Cambridge, 1972), and *An Essay on Theological Method* (Montana, 1975).

11. Kaufman, *An Essay on Thological Method, op. cit.,* p. 71.

PART II
THE ORIGINS
OF
CHRISTIAN CONSCIOUSNESS

II
The Emergence of
Human Consciousness

It is surprising how few theologians have studied the phenomenon of the "axial age" and pointed out its implications for
an understanding of Christianity. If, as some have maintained,
this was the age when genuine humanity both emerged and was
discovered, then pursuing the theme of how Christianity is related to this phenomenon would seem to be a particularly fruitful field of inquiry.[1] Broadly speaking, I suppose, we could
conceive of two theological points of view about the axial
period, falling on the two ends of a continuum. One would see
no particular theological significance in the axial age. This,
because theology has to do with God's revelation to man, not
with man's development in consciousness. To view Christianity
as a genuine part of the axial age would seem to deny that
Christ is the miraculous gift of God, the beginning of Paul's
"new creation" (2 Cor. 5:17; Eph. 2:15; Gal. 6:15) and in no
way the result of human evolution. The alternative view, the
one championed by Karl Jaspers,[2] equally sees no theological
significance in the axial age. But whereas the former view results from a theological supernaturalism, this latter view results
from an existentialist humanism. The axial age is to be accounted for in evolutionary, and thus this-worldly, terms. Jesus
might meaningfully be seen as a part of the axial age, but then
this means that he can be accounted for in human and evolutionary terms. There is no warrant here for invoking the supernatural. Both views, it seems to me, are based on the same assumptions about the supernatural and the natural, God and
man, grace and evolution. A more fruitful approach is one that
questions those very assumptions and sees no necessary opposition between an "evolutionary" explanation of Christianity and
one born from the desire to see in it the unexpected grace of

God. I do not intend to pursue this issue any further, except to point out that I wish to align myself with those thinkers who are of a common mind with Piet Schoonenberg:

> Moreover it is becoming ever more clear that the mistake of both parties lay not primarily in what each defended, nor even in attacks on one another, but much more in an implicit presupposition on which they were of one mind. This was that the truths which both adhered to needed to be reconciled. That means that Creator and created are rivals, that God's activity is at the cost of man and that man's freedom and originality are at the cost of God's causality, that God is less active where man is more so and vice versa.[3]

From this perspective, if the axial age was indeed a period where man was most active, then we possess an important index for discerning the precise configuration which "God's activity" took. To think differently is to hold the view that God and man are competitors, a view which, to my mind, comes from the Enlightenment polemics against religion, and which cannot be resolved so long as the problem is entered into on the Enlightenment's terms.

The Nature of the Axial Period in Recent Thought

If, as I proposed in my introduction, the development of man's consciousness determines what he can conceive as a genuine possibility for himself, then an understanding of man's consciousness in the axial period—the period of Jesus, among others—may aid us in conceiving what genuine possibility Jesus represented to axial men. The term "axial period" was used by Karl Jaspers[4] in 1949 to refer to the centuries between 800 B.C. and 200 B.C., a period in which a new kind of thinking arose in five parts of the Eurasian continent: in China with Confucius and Lao-tzu, in India with Gautama Buddha, in Persia with Zoroaster, in Greece with Thales, Pythagoras, Socrates and Plato, and in Israel with the prophetic movement.

Although Jaspers excludes Jesus from the axial period and seems to have chosen the term precisely to challenge the Christian contention that Jesus is the axis of history, nonetheless it is sufficient for our purposes at the moment that he does include Jesus in an indirect way: "From an historical viewpoint Jesus was the last in the series of Jewish prophets and stood in conscious continuity to them."[5]

Jaspers' own description of the axial period is almost lyrical, and deservedly so if he is correct. As he puts it:

What is new about this age . . . is that man becomes conscious of being as a whole, of himself and his limitations. He experiences the terror of the world and his own powerlessness. He asks radical questions. Face to face with the void, he strives for liberation and redemption. By consciously recognizing his limits he sets himself the highest goals. He experiences absoluteness in the depths of selfhood and in the lucidity of transcendence.

Consciousness became once more conscious of itself; thinking became its own object.

In this age were born the fundamental categories within which we still think today, and the beginnings of the world religions, by which human beings still live, were created. The step into universality was taken in every sense.[6]

In sum, we could say that for Jaspers what makes this period the "axis" of human history, even *our own* history today, is the fact that man emerged as an "individual" in the proper sense at this time: "These paths are widely divergent in their conviction and dogma, but common to all of them is man's reaching out beyond himself by growing aware of himself within the whole of Being and the fact that he can tread them only as an individual on his own."[7] Or, as he more summarily puts it: "What was later called reason and personality was revealed for the first time during the axial period."[8]

According to John Cobb,[9] relying on Jaspers, what lies at the basis of the axial period is the increasing role that rationality came to have at this time. This meant several things. First, with the increasing place that rationality came to have in man's psychic life, the power of mythical thinking was gradually superseded. Mythical thinking is governed by "projection," fantasy, and wish fulfillment. As rationality becomes more dominant in man's psychic life, it brings with it the ability to control, to check, and even to overturn mythical thinking through rational learning from experience. The Homeric critique of Greek religion, the prophetic critique of Canaanite polytheism, and the Buddha's critique of Brahmanic Hinduism are instances of this process of rationalization.

Second, a new sense of what it is to be an individual arose. Ontologically, of course, everyone is an individual, not only because he is not simply an exact replica of everyone else, but because of his ability to preserve his identity through an awareness of time. When one is aware of the succession of time, he is able to grasp that it is the same "I" who has acted in the past, is acting now, and will act in the future. This is why we still say today that someone who lacks an awareness of his past lacks an "identity." If such were possible, it would mean that he has had no chance to grasp the "continuous" and identical "I" underlying his various acts of the past. However, with the emergence of axial man, we have a new awareness of autonomy and thus identity making itself known. For the break from mythical thinking presupposes the ability to subject reality to one's own conscious control. The person as a subject emerges. Mythical thinking does not know the difference between subject and object, for projection is precisely characterized by the inability to make that distinction. It is this new experience of subjectivity that causes Jaspers to say that personality was revealed for the first time in this period. Cobb is equally as strong: "Hence, I am arguing also that the emergence of axial man was not only the emergence of a new understanding of man as individual, but of a new individuality."[10]

Third, a new sense of freedom emerged. Again, if by freedom one means spontaneity, the open-ended character of life, and the necessarily contingent character of existence, then, of course, pre-axial man was necessarily "free." But with the emergence of axial man, a new freedom arises. For when rationality comes to occupy the center of man's psychic life, then necessarily a new ability to subject oneself to one's own conscious and deliberate control emerges. Mythical thinking, with its lack of a distinction between subject and object, simply could not foster the kind of freedom meant by deliberate control. Because it lacked a sense of the "autonomous I," and thus "free I," it fostered a more passive image of man. We find a good example of the latter in Egyptian wisdom literature, where the contrast is often made between the "passionate man" and the "silent man."[11] It is the "silent man" who is extolled, for he is precisely the one who will not disrupt reality by changing it. In this mythical world of thought, "freedom" has not yet emerged as a value in itself.

In sum, Jaspers provides us with a neat summary of what was emerging in this period:

> This overall modification of humanity may be termed spiritualization. The unquestioned grasp on life is loosened, the calm of polarities becomes the disquiet of opposites and antinomies. Man is no longer enclosed within himself. He becomes uncertain of himself and thereby open to new and boundless possibilities. He can hear and understand what no one had hitherto asked or proclaimed. The unheard-of becomes manifest. Together with his world and his own self, Being becomes sensible to man, but not with finality: the question remains.[12]

Quite clearly, of course, the first question we must put to ourselves, before any attempt to explore the Christian implications of this period, is whether Jaspers' "axial period" is a valid notion. In this light, it may help to explore both the advantages and the necessary limits of this notion. In this regard, it seems important to call attention to the work of Eric Voegelin,[13] for curiously few have done as much as Voegelin both to critique Jaspers' notion of an "axial period" and yet to provide strong evidence for its validity.

First, Voegelin throughout all of his work has maintained that a break from mythical thinking did in fact occur, though, unlike Jaspers, he holds that the period in which this first occurred runs from Cyrus' conquest of Media in 550 B.C. to the decline of the Roman Empire in 546 A.D. This period is important to Voegelin precisely because it is that of the "ecumenic" or, we might say, intercultural empires (Babylon, Egypt, Persia, Macedonia, Rome, Greek and Phoenician city states, Maurya and Parthian empires, Israel and the Bactrian kingdoms; additionally, the period is extensive enough to include Christ, an omission quite glaring in Jaspers). The results of this period were both "pragmatic" and "spiritual." Pragmatically, the imperial conquests resulted in the need for a huge power organization, but a spiritual basis was lacking to give it meaning. One response to this was an "outburst of universal spirituality which in turn formed movements in search of a people whose order they could become."[14] This was the spiritual dimension, which resulted in what Voegelin terms "noetic" and "pneumatic" differentiation, which approximates Jaspers' philosophical and spiritual breakthrough of the axial period.

Second, however, Voegelin has always maintained some reservations about the axial period, whatever the dates one may assign to it, and in his latest work he at least concludes that the notion needs to be complemented by an awareness of history's recurrent lapse from the axis:

At the present state of experiential analysis, I conclude, the concept of an epoch or axis-time marked by the great spiritual outbursts alone is no longer tenable. Something "epochal" has occurred indeed; there is no reason why the adjective should be denied to the disintegration of the compact experience of the cosmos and the differentiation of the truth of existence. But the "epoch" involves, besides the spiritual outbursts, the ecumenic empires from the Atlantic to the Pacific and engenders the consciousness of history as the new horizon that surrounds with its divine mystery the existence of man in the habitat that has been opened by the concupiscence of power and knowledge.[15]

His first reservations were of a less drastic nature. He acknowledged the difference between Jaspers' more historically conscious approach to world history and the previous views of St.

Paul, Augustine, Bossuet, Voltaire, Spengler, and Hegel. Voltaire delivered a decisive blow to the Christian view by pointing out its failure to acknowledge the breakthrough of, for example, China and the Arab world. But Voltaire, and Spengler and Hegel as well, were not sufficiently historically conscious, claiming too much for their views: "When finite speculation possesses itself of the meaning of history . . . existence in historical form has ceased."[16] Voegelin credited Jaspers with breaking out of the European parochialism of previous thinkers, with tolerance for the different ways in which mankind searches for truth, and with a sensitivity for man's ability to fall from the gains of the axial period. His only early reservation was that "while the parallelisms are duly recognized, neither the problem of the successive leaps in being within the various societies, nor the problem of their differences of rank, has been worked through."[17]

So far Voegelin seemed willing to work with the notion of an axial period, at least in a critical way. However, in his latest work Voegelin wants to break from the neat delineation of periods and types of order characteristic of his earlier writings. An axial period seems to lend credence to a "periodical" or unilinear view of history, but the empirical data seem to point to innumerable and recurrent lapses back into a "pre-axial" mode of understanding. The naiveté and dogmatism characteristic of mythical thinking seems to find recurrent "equivalences" in modern man, wherever imperialism manifests itself, whether philosophically or politically. As Voegelin poignantly expresses it: "The constancies and equivalences adumbrated work havoc with such settled topical blocks as myth and philosophy, natural reason and revelation, philosophy and religion, or the Orient with its cyclical time and Christianity with its linear history."[18] Whether this means that the notion of an axial period should entirely be done away with, or should rather be complemented by a corresponding view of man's lapse back into archaism, seems unclear in Voegelin's thought.

Quite clearly Voegelin's target is a unilinear view of history, a view which envisions history as an inevitable process of progress and ever better differentiation, culminating in fulfillment. However, even Voegelin admits some historical progress, both in his affirmations of the "epochal" nature of the noetic and pneumatic differentiations, and in his clearly eschatological view of history. His contribution to Jaspers' "axial period" notion can perhaps be expressed as follows. First, it cannot be used as an argument in support of a unilinear conception of history. Second, the notion is too imprecise to actually account for all the differences in context and meaning of the various cultures involved. It is this latter which leads Voegelin to abandon the notion, for as he puts it: "The 'axis-time,' I had to conclude, was the symbolism by which a modern thinker tried to cope with the disturbing problem of meaningful structures in history, such as the field of parallel spiritual movements, of which the actors in the field were quite unaware."[19] But this having been said, what I think Voegelin's critique leads to is not an abandonment of the notion, but the recognition of its inherent limitations. As Benjamin Schwartz put it: "Like all periodization schemes that draw distinctions between one age and another age, the notion of the 'axial age' should be treated as a heuristic notion."[20]

I am convinced that Voegelin substantially agrees with Jaspers in finding in the first millennium evidence to support a fundamental maturation in human development. Voegelin's "noetic" and "pneumatic" differentiations are structurally equivalent to Jaspers' notion of "spiritualization." The most that could be said, I think, is that Jaspers focuses on what is common to the axial peoples, while Voegelin's predilection is for their differences. Voegelin's difficulties seem to stem not from any inherent difficulties with the fundamental breakthroughs that Jaspers articulates, but from inferences that are often drawn from those for a general philosophy of history. For example, the term "axial" might seem to presuppose a knowledge of universal history. How could one really know what is the axis of humanity unless he were capable of surveying the total sweep of human history? It is against this kind of Gnosticism that Voegelin inveighs.

Owing to the possibility of Voegelin's fear of Gnosticism in the notion of an axial period, it must be said that Eric Weil has made a significant contribution to our subject in his clarification of just what is meant by the "breakthroughs" of the first millennium.[21] We have used the term "breakthrough" before, and Weil seems to prefer it to Jaspers' term "axial." Clearly it does not carry the Gnostic overtones of the word "axial."

Weil is quite agreed with Jaspers and Voegelin in their view that something of decisive historical importance occurred in the first millennium. His contribution lies in precising what we mean by "decisive." First, of course, historical studies make it clear or at least probable that the axial leaders—Confucius, Buddha, the Greek philosophers, the prophets and Jesus —were not particularly decisive for their own contemporaries. Plato's views on society, as formulated in his *Laws* and *Republic,* did not find acceptance in Athenian society. The prophetic protest against legalism never seemed fundamentally to alter Jewish society, even to the time of Jesus. Jesus' own condemnation shows clearly that he was not accorded a decisive importance in his own time. Similarly, the evidence is clear from the start that the axial thinkers, far from being accorded an axial or decisive importance by their contemporaries, were considered the leaders of despised and persecuted groups. What, of course, kept the axial leaders from being accorded decisive importance by their contemporaries was the minority status of their movements. As Weil indicates, time was required before the small groups inspired by the individual axial geniuses could become mass movements. Greek thought had first to inspire men like Alexander the Great and Marcus Aurelius, the prophetic movement needed its St. Paul, and Buddhism needed its King Asoka before they could become decisive.

Second, then, what makes the axial leaders decisive is the fact that they were "successful." But there are different kinds of successes. There are successes which seem to have no lasting effect upon the course of history—to wit, as Weil mentions them, the Assyrians, the Huns, the Mongols, and the Germanic tribes. But some successes endure, and are decisive for later history. Why? Weil's answer is simple and yet convincing: because we ourselves accord them a decisive status. As he puts it:

. . . the history we write is always at bottom our own intellectual and political autobiography, an attempt to come

to a genetic understanding of our own way of living, acting, and feeling. The meanings of terms such as
"breakthrough" and "axial time" become clear only if we
use them in this context, if we acknowledge that the importance of events and dates is determined by the place we
assign to them in our autobiography, and not by their material weight. Any fact is as good as any other so long as
we adhere to a plan by which facts are merely defined as
that which existed in the past. On that level, the idea of
permanence, importance, and value becomes meaningless.
The men and teachings that figure in our collection of
"what is great in our past" occupy places of honor precisely because they are milestones on the way leading to ourselves, to what we regard as essential in our character,
morals, sentiments, and style: they are pieces in our (re)-
collection.[22]

Thus, the decisiveness of the axial period results from the fact
that we ourselves recognize still today the import of rationality,
of individuality, and of freedom in our own lives. Because authentic life seems impossible to us without these, we recognize
the axial period as a genuinely decisive breakthrough in human
history. That, it seems to me, is a sufficiently modest appraisal
of the axial period, and one which avoids the view of history
which Voegelin so rightly rejects. It in no way implies a knowledge of the total sweep of history, but only a recognition of
several factors which we ourselves deem central for our own
authentic existence.

The Axial Period from a Developmental Perspective

Thus far in our analysis, two principles of decisive import
for our study have emerged. First, the stage of development
reached by axial man generated a new consciousness or self-
awareness. Second, this new self-awareness determined what
axial man could imagine as a genuine possibility for himself.
The axial stage of development was characterized by the dominant role of rationality in man's life, which generated what

could be called a rational consciousness. Further, this rational consciousness in turn opened up an horizon of new possibilities for axial man, insofar as he could imagine himself as an individual in a new way, with a new kind of autonomous freedom. Several scholars have noted the important correlation between stages of development and human consciousness, and in my opinion it seems to offer an adequate account of how the axial period emerged.[23] At the same time, understanding this correlation will be of capital import for our study, insofar as it will provide us with a heuristic tool for understanding what kind of development and corresponding consciousness Christianity itself might represent.

A developmental perspective, then, links consciousness to the "texture" or level of one's development. That this is true on an individual level seems generally admitted now, since the refinements of Piaget and Kohlberg on genetic theories of human development.[24] Kohlberg's studies have led him to differentiate three levels of human development: pre-conventional, conventional, and post-conventional. Each level generates and presupposes a certain capacity of consciousness or self-awareness, which determines what the individual can imagine as a genuine human possibility. For example, what characterizes the "child" is dwelling in the immediate. The child's first experience is that of the "here and now." Since that is the only world he knows, he cannot be expected to have the more "expanded awareness" characteristic of the adolescent and the adult. This is why Kohlberg terms this stage "pre-conventional," meaning by this the kind of awareness which results when one's experience is not sufficiently broad to include the "conventions" of others— other individuals, groups, or societies. When a child hears the word "man," the meaning of that term is necessarily determined by the capacities which he possesses. If his here and now experience includes two men—his father and his uncle—then "man" means just that. "Man" cannot refer to mankind at large, simply because the child is incapable of such an abstraction at his limited stage of development. First, he will have to move beyond the "here and now" before the meaning of an abstraction can become clear to him. Similarly on a moral level —analysis of which is Kohlberg's contribution—what counts as

a "value" to the child is "immediate," "here and now" fulfillment. Avoiding a course of action because its long-term effects
might be debilitating simply doesn't "register" with the child.
Anyone who has seen a child touch a hot iron knows that.
Thinking about long-term effects requires the capacity to transcend the "here and now," and such is what the child cannot
do. John Dunne brings home the point rather well:

> The child is protected from evil by his immediacy. If he is
> hurt, he will cry, but he can go quickly from tears to
> smiles and laughter, forgetting the hurt in the small span
> of his awareness, when something pleasurable is placed
> before him.[25]

Hopefully, what emerges from this is the linkage between the
child's level of development—restriction to the here and now—
and his corresponding "immediate" self-awareness. The child's
horizon of possibilities is largely circumscribed by that.

What characterizes the shift from childhood to "adolescence" is an enlargement in the child's development beyond the
immediate. This begins in an inchoate way, as the child learns
that his parents are not simply extensions of its own ego. Every
time the parent says "no" to the child, he glimpses a difference
between himself and the parent. His world begins to widen as
he learns that another world exists beyond that of the immediate one of his own wants and needs. Kohlberg speaks of this as
the "conventional" phase, and it can be said to begin when the
"conventions" of others become the controlling factors in the
child's life. Intellectually the adolescent is aware of worlds of
thought other than the immediate one of his dreams and
aspirations—the world of his friends and enemies, the world of
his schoolmates, the world opened up by literature and history.
Morally what counts as a value begins to shift from his own
immediate satisfaction to what is approved by others—first, of
course, to what is approved by his friends, but as his entrance
into society deepens, the values upheld by his society at large
will largely determine his value system. Dunne refers to this as
the "existential" phase, because now the adolescent's "existence" becomes problematic: others threaten him, force him to

ask questions, challenge his childhood views, etc. Again, what emerges from this is the linkage between the adolescent's stage of development and his corresponding awareness or consciousness. The latter is not ready-made, but only emerges as the child's development calls for an expansion in his own conscious capacities.

Kohlberg's third level, which, according to his studies, few reach, marks a further advance in development and consciousness. He characterizes this as "post-conventional" insofar as the determining factor in an "adult's" psychic life is no longer necessarily the "conventions" of a particular society, but what the adult understands to be true or valuable in itself. Intellectually and morally a person is now self-principled, and we can speak here of the emergence of the full and autonomous person. The person no longer simply echoes the ideas and values of others, but is a self, with a capacity to distance himself from and evaluate the views of others. Jung would refer to this as the "individuated" person, while Dunne prefers the term "historic," insofar as the adult has transcended simple self- and societal interest and committed himself to what is inherently valuable and thus applicable to historic man at large.

What especially characterizes this post-conventional level is an intensification in the ability to abstract. This abstractive ability was already present in the conventional phase, for the socialization process occurring then required of the individual that he appreciate the existence of groups and social entities. These latter are not simply concrete realities, immediately tangible to the senses, but abstractions discerned by the mind. Both Piaget and Kohlberg have noted that this abstractive ability intensifies as the person's experience complexifies, and I think that the element of complexification is the key to understanding abstraction. A simple example might make the point better. A "grunt" is not an abstraction. It is a concrete utterance whose significance is tied to its immediate context. It could mean that one is content after a filling meal. It could also mean that one is uncomfortable. The point is that its meaning can only be known from the concrete context. An abstraction's function, however, is precisely to free the person from the immediate and concrete context. "Society" as an ab-

straction transcends the here and now context and its meaning
is graspable apart from the concrete context. It is a creation of
the mind resulting from the person's greater complexity of experience. That more complexified experience has enabled the
person to grasp relationships between innumerable concrete experiences, relationships which transcend all of them. This is
precisely the function of an abstraction.

Now, on the post-conventional level this abstractive ability
is further intensified. For the post-conventional person has not
only distanced himself from (abstracted from) his immediate
and concrete contexts, but he has distanced himself from societal values also. His activity is characterized by the desire to
define what is true and valuable in itself—universally—apart
from whether his society or any society proclaims any such
truth or value. This is an intensified use of abstraction, for one
is attempting to grasp not simply what characterizes a particular society, but what characterizes all societies.

Again, the element of complexification is the key factor
underlying the emergence of this intensified abstractive ability.
According to Kohlberg, three further factors have complexified
the person's world. First, there is the factor of skepticism
which ensues because of a conflict in the values held by the
various groups or societies in the person's experience. Should
this kind of conflict occur, the individual will be led to question
the reasons bringing this about. His naiveté about society will
diminish. Values he once might have thought to be absolute
will appear increasingly relative—"relative," that is, to the interested groups or societies. Second, Kohlberg speaks of the
factor of "egoism," and what he has in mind is that, as the individual begins to grasp the inadequacy of societal values, he is
forced back upon himself. He must increasingly rely upon his
own critical and reasoning ability. Should he do so he will discover the value of reason itself and thereby discover his own
autonomy. Finally, the new experience of relativism will lead
him either to a cynical view of human life or to a new discovery
of values upon which he can meaningfully base his life. The
first alternative would ultimately destroy the new sense of autonomy he has gained. It is because of this that, as Kohlberg
postulates, the post-conventional individual begins to develop

the notion of universal principles and ideals, which can give meaning to every man's life as well as adjudicate differences between conflicting value claims.

What emerges from Kohlberg's analyses is an insight into the nature of human development. A number of factors, to which we will return, stand out. Human development is a process of complexification and differentiation. In the movement from childhood to adulthood we notice an increasing expansion of "worlds"—from the immediate world, to the wider world mediated by society, to the world of critical reflection and self-principled behavior. This expansion complexifies the person's life, but it is also the condition for the emergence of new and thus differentiated capacities. Immediacy brings forth the capacities of wonder, awe, security, fantasy, dreaming, and projecting. Adolescence calls for an increasing autonomy, a social consciousness, and the beginnings of a critical awareness. Adulthood brings with it individuation, a sense of autonomy, self-principled behavior, and a full development of one's critical and rational faculties. Further, this process is not irreversible or inevitable. Each new phase of development is a "breakthrough" occasioned by the "breakdown" of the previous phase, but the very factors that can lead to a breakthrough can also inhibit it, for with increasing complexification comes increasing confusion or lack of orientation. Rather than working through this problem, the person can respond by regressing to a previous phase of development. Hence, I prefer the term "development" to "evolution." The latter has a ring of irreversibility to it. Further, it is a gradual process marked by both continuity and discontinuity. While each new differentiation may seem like a quantum leap, it nonetheless only emerges because of the previous phases of development. A differentiation is not the discovery of something totally new, but the intensification and increasing dominance of capacities latent in the person. The element of continuity is the "ego" of the child itself. The element of discontinuity is the differentiation that ego gradually undergoes. Finally, this process is not linear, but one of "sublation." Previous phases of development are not completely left behind, but are integrated into a higher synthesis. The capacities called forth by adulthood oc-

cupy a dominant role in his life, but they do not completely
eradicate the capacities of previous phases of development.
Thus, it is always possible to regress to a previous phase. The
regression can be beneficial if the person returns from the reversion enriched by what it had to offer. This is a kind of
"regression in the service of the ego," and adults engage in it
when they enjoy the childhood capacities of fantasy, wonder,
and awe. It becomes destructive, however, if a return is
"blocked," as when an adult cannot break away from the fantasy world he has created.

Kohlberg's analysis provides us with a heuristic tool for
deciphering what is involved in individual human development.
As such, it is at a high level of abstraction, and does not pur-
port to describe the many variations of human development
which exist in the concrete. However, it is very valuable insofar
as it provides us with a tool for decoding recurrent aspects of
human development. One of its most valuable aspects for us is
that we can use it as a tool for deciphering cultural development as well. What is involved in this further move is an extrapolation from our own understanding of individual development to the level of cultural development. There is nothing new
in this, insofar as all history is written from our own point of
view. That is what Freud did, for example, when he extrapolated from his interpretation of individual patients' histories to
that of history at large.[26] To my mind, the notion of extrapolation was not incorrect. Rather, what he extrapolated with—his
understanding of the Oedipus complex—restricted his ability to
adequately account for all of the known cultural and historical
data.

Generalizing, then, a view of individual human development into one of cultural development at large, we can speculate that what characterized "primitive" man was a kind of immediacy or pre-conventional consciousness. Lévy-Bruhl has
described this as the "participation mystique":

Participation mystique may be said to be a mysterious in-
terchange or continuity between separate entities because
they are psychologically identified with one another. For
the primitive man, like the very young child, has no defi-

nite boundaries to his psyche—everything that happens is both in himself and in the object; he feels with the animals, the trees, and so forth. . . . Before the "I," the *autos,* has been established as a center of individual awareness, the child has no personal consciousness, but exists in a condition of identification with his surroundings. This state of affairs is to be seen particularly clearly in the infant's relation to the mother. He lives in complete *participation* with her, and she is related to him in a similar way though to a lesser degree. Even after he leaves her womb, the infant is still entirely dependent on her and so partakes of both her physical and her psychological condition. After the child's physical dependence has been outgrown, this identity with the mother persists as a psychological reality. For in the unconscious the psyches of mother and child have no clear dividing lines. He is contained psychologically within her all-embracing protection until he has won his freedom and his psychological independence.[27]

As a child's development is limited by his immediate, here-and-now environment, we can speculate with Lévy-Bruhl that such a limitation to the immediate and natural environment characterized earliest man. Dunne hints at the same idea: "Probably there was a time when man was much closer to the other animals, when men and women were immediate and spontaneous like children."[28] This means that man would have understood himself in the light of nature, his immediate context. Richardson calls this the "mimetic consciousness," in which man imitates or "mimes" nature. A particularly intriguing example, suggested by Richardson, is human sacrifice:

Primitive human sacrifice was one aspect of this *mimesis.* In human sacrifice, as in the yearly death and rebirth of vegetation, a part of the species is caused to die so that the species itself may survive. Human sacrifice is man's way of seeking to live "mimetically," by imitating nature.[29]

For our purposes, this kind of analysis enables us to understand the role that mythical thinking played in the life of primitive man. Since primitive man dwelled in a kind of immediacy with nature, this means that he had not yet developed a clear understanding of himself as distinct from nature. The difference between subject and object had not yet clearly emerged. Because of this, he was incapable of determining the difference between external reality and his own subjective understanding. Object and subject, the external and the internal, were a kind of undifferentiated whole. Thus, we would say today that mythical thinking is characterized by "projection," which is precisely the inability to distinguish external reality and one's own subjective views of the former. Further, because primitive man "mimed" nature, he quite spontaneously ascribed to his projections the same reality that nature had for him. The gods, of whatever kind, were as real as nature itself. This miming of nature also led to a veneration of nature, the so-called "numinous" mentality, in which nature appears as the sacred reality determining man's destiny. Finally, the presence of mythical thinking enables us further to comprehend the difference between man, even at this stage, and animal life. For mythical thinking at least presupposes man's capacity to transcend merely biological needs—the survival of the body, the key aim of animal life—and aim at some kind of psychic satisfaction.[30]

As adolescence marks both an expansion in the child's world and a transition to adulthood, we can further speculate that the race as a whole—in its representatives—went through a similar development. Utilizing Kohlberg, I think we can speak of a cultural conventional consciousness, inasmuch as what characterized this transitional age was a gradual entry into a kind of conventionalized or community-oriented existence. The hunting and food-gathering of primitive man did not lend itself to the settling and thus conventionalizing of communities. It was more nomadic and unstable, oriented more to the immediate needs of the moment, rather than the longer-term planning necessitated by settled life. However, with the domestication of animals and the cultivation of plants, we can speak of a first entry into conventionalized life. This, of course, would call for a greater degree of planning and organizing on men's part. With the emergence of city life and civilization in the fourth millennium, we can speculate that the entry into conventionalized life had reached its peak.

What is important for us is what the great civilizations represent in terms of human development. Life in Mesopotamia, India, China, Mexico and Peru called for new capacities on men's part, the most important of which was engaging in a great deal of rational planning. The development of the legal codes may be taken as exemplifications of this. Thus, we could say that this period was marked by the increasing rationalization of man's psychic capacities. Rationalization, unlike mythical thinking, called for planning, checking, and appraising one's ideas in the light of their actual effectiveness. Two psychic capacities of man began to exist in tension: mythical and rational thinking. Dunne sees the latter especially in the invention of writing; it "had to be invented; it could not be discovered like a natural process."[31] Such an invention was not just a discovery of a new tool; it was a discovery of men's rational abilities themselves. We can, of course, only speculate as to why the discovery of rational thinking could not yet overcome the predominance of myth in the ancient civilizations. Perhaps Dunne is not wide of the mark when he thinks that man's new power filled him with fear, in the face of which the security of the myth seemed all the more necessary: "From this point on in pre-history, as in life itself, happiness must have become a much more difficult thing to attain; it must have seemed to man that he had been excluded from the garden of paradise, that he must earn his bread in the sweat of his brow."[32]

Along with Jaspers, Voegelin, and Cobb, we can account for the axial period by positing that the increasing use of rational thinking led to its dominance over mythical thinking sometime in the first millennium B.C. Once rational thinking was discovered, it must have embodied an immensely potent value in itself. We can easily understand this if we remember the three factors implied in rational thought, to which we referred earlier. The break from mythical thinking was the first factor. While myth was a way in which man gave meaning to his world, nonetheless it implied a certain subservience of man to nature. The discovery of reason meant in principle that man could reverse the relationship: man does not simply yield to nature; nature yields to him. Hence the increased sense of autonomous individuality and freedom, the second and third factors. The Greek philosophers' demythologization of the pantheon, the Buddha's critique of Brahmanic Hinduism with its supposed irreversible caste system, Zoroaster's critique of early Aryan religion, and the prophetic critique of early Judaism—all were breaks from the "mythical" order of nature, and thus intense experiences of human individuality and freedom. With Kohlberg, we can say that what emerged, in principle, was a human "post-conventional consciousness." For now man defined himself, not in terms of nature, nor in terms of the conventions of groups or societies, but in terms of himself.

Again, what we should notice in the axial period is the intensification of abstraction. Already in mankind's conventional phase, the process of socialization underlying this demanded a great amount of abstraction. The conventional legal codes, for example, required the conceiving of societal values and intergroup relationships. As Piaget and Kohlberg pointed out, these latter required abstraction, for they were not immediately tangible to the senses. Early man's experience had first to be complexified through socialization before more perceptive individuals could grasp the kinds of complex societal interrelationships expressed in the legal codes. Now what characterizes the axial period is that this power of abstraction had become developed enough so as to call into question the mythical vision underlying the civilizations of man up to that time. Very likely each of the axial leaders underwent a process structurally equivalent to that which Kohlberg maintains the post-conventional individual passes through today—a process, that is, involving skepticism, egoism, and relativism.

Skepticism ensues from the awareness of conflicts in values between various societal groups and even between societies themselves. The conflict between the various Hindu castes very likely led Buddha to his own radical skepticism about Brahmanic Hinduism itself. The emerging international empires of the first millennium, with their conflicting claims, probably fostered a similar skepticism in the minds of some. What were once thought to be absolute claims began to appear as relative to the societies or empires which generated them. As each of the axial leaders became aware of the inadequacies of the various conflicting societies, he was forced inward, through which he discovered the power of his own rationality. Precisely because he could call society into question, he discovered his own autonomy. It is at this point that the mythical naiveté broke down. This could have led to a radical skepticism and relativism, but in the case of the axial leaders it led to a new and universal vision of mankind. Apart from the differences in these various visions, my interest at this point is in signalizing the intensification in reason or abstraction. For in his own way, each of the axial leaders found himself capable of abstracting from the values of society, distancing himself from them and subjecting them to a critique.

The axial period, then, marks the culmination of a long process of human complexification and differentiation. What we can notice is an increasing expansion of "worlds," from the immediate and mythical world of primitive man, to the conventional and thus increasingly rationalized world of the great civilizations, to the post-conventional world of axial man. This "expansion" provides the conditions for the emergence of capacities: early man's use of myth, the increasing role of rationalization in civilizational man, and the breakthrough to complete individuation in axial man. This is as far as Jaspers goes, for in principle, with the breakthrough to individuation, Jaspers can envisage nothing greater. Potentially, at least, rationality can account for everything that has emerged in the history of man subsequent to the axial age. And yet we have noticed that Voegelin, Cobb, and even Toynbee criticize Jaspers for not clearly distinguishing the differences between the axial leaders. He stresses what is common to them, but it is now time to query their possible differences.

Actually it would require an expert in Buddhism, Confucianism, Taoism, Zoroastrianism, classical Greek thought, Judaism and Christianity adequately to distinguish the differences between these very complicated axial traditions. What I have to say here is only meant by way of a proposal to the various experts in these fields. Only they are in a position to assess the merits of the matter.

Frankly, I see great merit in Voegelin's distinction between what he terms the breakthrough to "philosophy," or, elsewhere, the "noetic" differentiation, and the "pneumatic" differentiation. The former, the noetic differentiation, would seem to characterize all the axial leaders. Benjamin Schwartz helpfully calls this "the strain toward transcendence":

> The word "transcendence" is a word heavy with accumulated meanings, some of them very technical in the philosophic sense. What I refer to here is something close to the etymological meaning of the word—a kind of standing back and looking beyond—a kind of critical, reflective questioning of the actual and a new vision of what lies beyond. It is symbolized in the Hebrew tradition by Abraham's departure from Ur and all it represents, by the Buddha's jen within and the normative orders without, by the Lao-tse book's strain toward the nameless *Tao,* and by the Greek strain toward an order beyond the Homeric gods, by the Socratic search within as well as by Orphic mysteries.[33]

So far so good. And yet we must ask, with Voegelin, whether the pneumatic differentiation does not introduce something quite radically "new" into man's existence. While we might say that each of the axial leaders broke through to ultimate principles of human existence, insofar as they no longer based life's meaning on immediate needs or the conventions of society but on truly post-conventional values—or ultimate principles of human existence—nonetheless there is one "ultimate" which seems to entail quite drastic revisions in human self-understanding. We are referring, of course, to the breakthrough to a demythologized and thus completely transcendent notion of God which characterizes some of the axial leaders. While probing the implications of this discovery is the key aim of this essay, still at this point I think it important to provide the reader with Voegelin's own views on the difference this differentiation can make:

> For the participation in being changes its structure when it becomes emphatically a partnership with God, while the participation in mundane being recedes to second rank. The more perfect attunement to being through conversion is not an increase on the same scale but a qualitative leap. And when this conversion befalls a society, the converted community will experience itself as qualitatively different from all other societies that have not taken the leap. Moreover, the conversion is experienced, not as the result of human action, but as a passion, as a response to a revelation of divine being, to an act of grace, to a selection for emphatic partnership with God. The community, as in the case of Israel, will be a chosen people, a peculiar people, a people of God.[34]

A further point to be made, however, is that the axial period was neither irreversible nor inevitable. I indicated earlier, in detailing the process of individual development, that each new phase marks a breakthrough occasioned by a previous breakdown. But the crucial point to underscore is that a breakthrough need not occur. The eventual collapse of the great civilizations can be taken as a sufficient indication of this. There is an element of freedom and creativity involved in properly human development, which holds good not only for individuals, but for whole cultures. It was because of this that Jaspers disclaimed the notion that the axial period represents "a universal stage in human evolution." In fact the term evolution is misleading if it connotes an irreversible trend in human history. As Jaspers claims, such a view overlooks "the clear fact that it was not mankind, not all men, who by that time had occupied the entire planet, but only a few, relatively very few, who took this step forward."[35] For this reason, I prefer to speak of human development rather than human evolution.

In this light, when we speak of the axial period as a breakthrough occasioned by a previous breakdown, we intend

to indicate, with Weil, that the breakdown "would be the necessary (not the sufficient) condition for the breakthrough."[36]
The element of the breakdown in Israel is perhaps well known
to us Christians: the destruction of the northern and southern
kingdoms and the consequent need to view their "God" not
simply as a national God, but as an absolute God who even
inspires Israel's enemies. Only in this way could Israel give
meaning to its current history. Again, the legalism rampant in
Jewish society at the time of Jesus might be viewed as a further
breakdown. Weil indicates the possible breakdowns of the
other axial cultures: the Greek need to give a positive meaning
to the "barbarians" who were quickly becoming Greek citi-
zens, the Chinese need for meaning in response to the "fighting
kingdoms," the senseless caste system with its ritualism, and
the warrior ideal in India. In each case we can perhaps pin-
point a breakdown, but, as Jaspers put it, "they are pre-condi-
tions of which the creative result is not a necessary sequel."[37]
Perhaps, in this light, too, we can assess the political factor of
the axial period as another "necessary but not sufficient" condition for the axis. Voegelin helpfully speaks of the pragmatic
ecumene emerging at this time. These new imperial orders
called for a spiritual ecumene to give them meaning. The previous national (read: conventional) understanding of man was
breaking down, and what was called for was a universal (read:
post-conventional) view. But by its very nature a spiritual ecumene must arise from man's freedom and creativity. Thus Voegelin's caveat: "The pressure of a historical situation" must
meet "with a sensitive and active mind."[38]

Third, the evidence indicates that we should view the axial
period as a gradual process, marked by both continuity and
discontinuity. Jaspers has been criticized for seeing it as wholly
unparalleled, and this can rightly be questioned. Just as we
maintained that in individual development the psychic capacity
of the ego provides the factor of continuity, so the evidence indicates a similar continuity in cultural development. It seems
best, then, to speak of an intensification or heightening of a capacity, rather than its emergence ex nihilo. In the case of the
axial period I would view the psychic capacity for rational

thinking as the basic element that was intensified by the axial leaders. This intensification could psychologically appear, however, as "unparalleled," if one thinks of the new forms of individuality and freedom that emerged. It could even appear as wholly beyond man's capacity, as it did in the case of Voegelin's "pneumatic differentiation." However, the element of continuity seems called for by the evidence. Weil lends confirmation to this in his contention that "a breakthrough happens only where and when it is admitted that the old way has led to a wall; but even then it will happen only if a turning is discovered that can be considered as prolonging the old way so that it does not become meaningless."[39] One of the main reasons that certain movements fail is precisely that they are too discontinuous, demanding capacities which in fact do not exist. An easily accessible example might be the extreme apocalypticism of Jesus' day, which Voegelin sees foreshadowed in the early Isaiah. What it demanded was world-escapism and a total transcendence of rationality. Finally, if we stress the "gradual" nature of the axial period, we can appreciate why Jaspers has been criticized for omitting Jesus, Mohammed, and Mahayana Buddhism from his "axial list." The gradual nature of the axis works both "backward" and "forward"—backward to the increasing development of rational thinking called for by the emerging civilizations; forward to the heightening of elements in rational thinking only dimly glimpsed by its earliest users.

Finally, the evidence indicates that the axial period forms part of a "sublationary" rather than a "linear" movement. The various differentiations of the axis do not annul, but presuppose and integrate, the various complexifications underlying them. Transactional analysis has popularized this notion by insisting that the fully integrated "adult" (post-conventional) is partly child (pre-conventional) and partly parent (conventional). We are simply generalizing this insight into a cultural dictum. Thus, we can always find pre-conventional and conventional elements in the axial leaders. The element of mythical-thinking, for example, stands out, and its presence in the axial leaders should lead us to suspect that it need not always be contradictory to rational thinking. We may have here an example, on the cultural level, of a "regression in the service of the ego."[40]

Notes

1. The most explicit treatment by a Christian theologian is John B. Cobb's superb *The Structure of Christian Existence* (Philadelphia, 1967), to which I shall return often. The only other theological treatments are Dunne and Richardson, *op. cit.* Each of these works has been highly influential on my own, as will become apparent.

2. Cf. Jaspers, *op. cit.*, which is the classical treatment of the "axial period." The scant attention paid to Jesus in that work has been somewhat corrected in *The Great Philosophers: The Foundations* (New York, 1962), pp. 74-106, where Jaspers views Jesus as one of humanity's "paradigmatic individuals."

3. Piet Schoonenberg, *The Christ* (New York, 1971), p. 16. Schoonenberg is representative of a large number of contemporary theologians. For a good overview, see David Tracy, *Blessed Rage for Order* (New York, 1975), pp. 22-42.

4. Jaspers, *op. cit.*, pp. 1-77.

5. *Ibid.*, p. 58.

6. *Ibid.*, p. 2.

7. *Ibid.*, p. 4.

8. *Ibid.*

9. Cobb, *op. cit.*, "Axial Existence," pp. 52-59.

10. *Ibid.*, p. 57.

11. G. Ernest Wright, *The Old Testament against Its Environment* (London, 1966), p. 44.

12. Jaspers, *op. cit.*, p. 3.

13. Cf. his brilliant *Order and History, op. cit.* Most important with respect to the axial period are Volume 2, *The World of the Polis*, pp. 1-24, and the whole of Volume 4, *The Ecumenic Age*, but especially pp. 1-58, where Voegelin calls into question his earlier assessment. Also helpful are Gerhart Niemeyer, "Eric Voegelin's Philosophy and the Drama of Mankind," *Modern Age* 20 (1976) 28-39; John Kirby, "Symbols and Dogmatics: Voegelin's Distinction," *The Ecumenist* 13 (1975) 26-31; and Frederick D. Wilhelmsen's review of Volume 4 in *Triumph* 10 (1975) 32-35.

14. Niemeyer, *art. cit.*, 32.

15. Voegelin, *op. cit.*, Vol. 4, pp. 312-313. For Voegelin, noetic differentiation is man's consciousness of his own finitude reaching out toward the infinite. "Gnosticism" ("concupiscence") is his favorite term for the failure to preserve the tension between the finite and infinite, and he sees this failure still occurring in all "dogmatic" systems; viz., "And what is modern about the modern mind, one may ask, if Hegel, Comte and Marx, in order to create an image of history that will support their ideological imperialism, still use the same techniques for distorting the reality of history as their Sumerian

predecessors?" (*ibid.*, p. 68). Niemeyer and Wilhelmsen both see this "Gnosticism" at work in Voegelin's own treatment of Christ, interestingly enough.

16. Voegelin, *op. cit.*, Vol. 2, p. 19.

17. *Ibid.*, p. 21 (Voegelin was especially critical of Jaspers' scant attention to Christ). Voegelin links Jaspers and the "late" Toynbee together. Volumes 7 to 10 of Toynbee's *Study of History* manifest a "reversal" of his thought, in which he accepts Jaspers' view in principle, but with two corrections: (1) the axis should be extended to include the disintegration of the Indian, Syriac, Sinic, and Hellenic civilizations, thus from the tenth century B.C. to the thirteenth century A.D., to include Mahayana Buddhism, Hinduism, Christianity, and Islam; (2) Jaspers too exclusively concentrates on the year 500 B.C. He does not sufficiently indicate that Buddha, Confucius, and Pythagoras were only chronological, not philosophical, contemporaries. Different conditions were operative in each.

18. Voegelin, *op. cit.*, Vol. 4, p. 68. This lapse into archaism is what he calls "historiogenesis," according to Thomas J. J. Altizer, "A New History and a New but Ancient God? A Review Essay," *Journal of the American Academy of Religion* 43 (1975) 758: "Historiogenesis is an ancient imperial creation, its intention being to sublimate the contingencies of imperial order in time to the timeless serenity of the cosmic order itself." Voegelin sees this process still at work; hence his refusal to view history in a periodic and unilinear manner. As he put it, lumping together hermeticism, Gnosticism, and alchemy—all forms of historiogenesis—in "Response to Altizer's 'A New History and a New but Ancient God?'" *Journal of the American Academy of Religion* 43 (1975) 769: "In our contemporary world, alchemist magic is primarily to be found among the ideologists who infest the social sciences with their efforts to transform man, society, and history."

19. *Ibid.*, p. 5.

20. Benjamin I. Schwartz, "The Age of Transcendence," *Daedalus* 104 (1975) 3.

21. Eric Weil, "What Is a Breakthrough in History?" *Daedalus* 104 (1975) 21-36. This entire issue, titled "Wisdom, Revelation, and Doubt: Perspectives on the First Millennium B.C.," is devoted to an analysis of the axial period.

22. *Ibid.*, 22-23.

23. Cf. Richardson, *op. cit.*, esp. p. 17, and Dunne, *op. cit.*, pp. 135-136.

24. Cf. Jean Piaget, *The Moral Judgment of the Child, op. cit.*, and Lawrence Kohlberg, "Stages of Moral Development as a Basis for Moral Education," C.M. Beck, ed., *Moral Education, Interdisciplinary Approaches* (New York, 1971), pp. 23-92. The advance of Piaget and Kohlberg beyond earlier genetic theories is in accounting for and yet transcending both psychological and sociological determinism through the role of human freedom and creativity in the developmental process.

25. Dunne, *op. cit.*, p. 144. Structurally equivalent to Kohlberg's stages is Dunne's own analysis of the child as "immediate man," the youth as "existential man," and the adult as "historic man" (cf. *ibid.*, pp. 46-47, 135-156, 157-163, 204-206).

26. Cf. Sigmund Freud, *Moses and Monotheism* (New York, 1955), *Totem and Taboo* (New York, 1952), and *Civilization and Its Discontents* (New York, 1962). A brief example of Freud's basis for extrapolating is found in his *A General Introduction to Psychoanalysis* (New York, 1953), pp. 209-210: "The era to which the dream-work takes us back is 'primitive' in

a twofold sense: in the first place, it means the early days of the individual—his childhood—and secondly, insofar as each individual repeats in some abbreviated fashion during childhood the whole course of the development of the human race, the reference is phylogenetic. . . . It seems to me that a symbolism, which the individual has not acquired by learning, may justly claim to be regarded as phylogenetic heritage."

27. As cited by Richardson, *op. cit.,* pp. 17-18.

28. Dunne, *op. cit.,* pp. 144-145.

29. Richardson, *op. cit.,* p. 5.

30. As Cobb, *op. cit.,* p. 39, puts it: ". . . we can say that at that point at which the surplus psychic energy became sufficient in quantity to enable the psychic life to become its own end rather than primarily a means to the survival and health of the body, the threshold was crossed dividing man from the animal. Man is that being in which the psyche aims at its own well-being."

31. Dunne, *op. cit.,* p. 146. Just as action precedes reflection, so the rationality of the conventional period is more pragmatic and action-oriented ("will-oriented"), whereas in the post-conventional period the reflective aspect of rationality predominates. Cf., on this, Neumann, *op. cit.,* pp. 126-127.

32. Dunne, *op. cit.,* p. 145.

33. Schwartz, *art. cit.,* 3.

34. Voegelin, *op. cit.,* Vol. 1, p. 10. I am not maintaining that man only arrived at a notion of the "absolute" in the axial period. Religious history points to the fact that even primitive man had his "absolutes." What I would suggest, however, is that man understood the "absolute" in a basically mythical way in the pre-conventional phase, in a mythico-rational way in the conventional phase, and in a demythologized way in the post-conventional (axial) phase. At least one recent study on the development of Hebraic monotheism seems to point to the same conclusion; cf. N. Nikiprowetzky, "Ethical Monotheism," *Daedalus* 104 (1975) 69-89. It should come as no surprise that a philosophically mature view of divine transcendence only emerged in the axial period, for the notion of "transcendence" requires a rational consciousness which is capable of abstracting beyond immediate sense experience and even beyond societal values—abstracting to a universal principle of reality. Further, while I agree with Heiler's view that all the world's high religions maintain an awareness of the "absolute," I would also hold that there are different kinds of awareness of this "absolute," and that a fully differentiated notion of divine transcendence issues forth in the sense of "grace" and "chosenness" indicated by Voegelin (cf. Friedrich Heiler, "The History of Religions as a Preparation for the Cooperation of Religions," M. Eliade and J. M. Kitagawa, eds., *The History of Religions: Essays in Methodology* [Chicago, 1949], p. 142). Finally, this developmental approach to revelation might make some uncomfortable, in that it seems to reduce the "revelation of the Old and New Testaments" to a discovery on man's part, rather than as God's gift. I would only maintain that it is possible for something to be both God's gift and man's discovery simultaneously, and that any other view is not a properly philosophical view of divine transcendence. Further, the designation of something as a "gift of God" is a second-order one—that is, a category created by men to describe a particular facet of an experience or differentiation of consciousness that they have undergone. That does not mean, however, that the category is incorrect.

35. Jaspers, *op. cit.*, p. 17 and p. 15.
36. Cf. Weil, *art. cit.*, 25, for what follows.
37. Jaspers, *op. cit.*, p. 18.
38. Voegelin, *op. cit.*, Vol. 1, p. 8.
39. Weil, *art. cit.*, 26-27.
40. There is a difference between the mythical thinking of a child and that of an adult. Both perceive "reality" as an undifferentiated whole, but in the case of the child this perception is uncritical, while in that of the adult it is demythologized and can lead to the so-called supra-conceptual, mystical, and higher states of consciousness. Cf. Robert E. Ornstein, *The Psychology of Consciousness* (San Francisco, 1972).

III
Christ and the Emergence of Christian Consciousness

Some Presuppositions

We have been considering the axial period as essentially one which marks a decisive turning point in the development of man. That turning point was reached when rational thinking, in principle, was able to break through the power of myth. This, in turn, fostered a new consciousness in man, the consciousness of individuality and freedom. We might say that human consciousness, properly so called, emerged at the axial period. Hence Jaspers' use of the term "axial." If human consciousness emerged, then it was our "axis" too. Our reason for the detailed study on the axial period was simply to provide us with the heuristic tools for probing the Christ and Christianity in a truly developmental way. What stage of human development, what corresponding consciousness, what consequent enlargement of human possibilities do we find represented by the Christ and Christianity?

So far as I know, two chief difficulties exist for the approach we are proposing here. One might be called the theological difficulty, and it has to do with a general attitude to theological issues in general, which spills over especially in the area of Christology. This view insists that theology has to do with God's revelation to man, not with man's discovery of God. Any attempt to describe theological realities from a human point of view must ultimately jeopardize the Christian belief that Christianity results from God's initiative. Moreover, this point is especially poignant when it comes to Christ, since here we are dealing with an event which is as unique and unpredictable as any historical event. It cannot be accounted for in human terms, for its very unpredictability manifests its divine origins. In response to this I would like to underline several points.

If this attitude is logically thought through, it reduces revelation to something fully extrinsic to and beyond man. One must then wonder what "revelation" really means, if it is in no way a reality that man discovers. What, then, is really "revealed" to man? That is why this attitude "generates" its opposite, the demise of God and revelation. If revelation is fully extrinsic to man, then why speak of revelation at all? But the further difficulty is more incisive, namely the pretension that man can ever speak from God's point of view. The denial of any human or this-worldly explanation of religious realities would demand that man can somehow transcend humanity and take God's own position. The ultimate difficulty would appear to be the implicit presupposition that a human explanation necessarily denies God's initiative. Since this is not a book on God, I cannot adequately deal with this question. I would, however, say two things. First, this presupposition comes from the Enlightenment's polemics against Christianity, which both Christians and non-Christians accepted, and there is no resolution of the problem as long as the Enlightenment's statement of the problem is accepted. Second, a human explanation for Christian realities does not necessarily deny God's initiative, but only makes clear that that God is not a mythical, "outsider" God who capriciously intervenes into human history.[1]

The other difficulty is hermeneutical and refers to the New Testament sources and the validity of our use of them. To some this axial interpretation of Christ and Christianity will appear to be an arbitrary example of eisegesis. One of the key aims of hermeneutical science is to articulate one's principles of interpretation, precisely so that their possible arbitrariness can be noticed and critiqued. Briefly, then, I would like to consider my own principles of interpretation.

As I understand it, three possible hermeneutical avenues exist. The first aims at reconstructing the layers of meaning and contexts behind or "implied" by the New Testament texts. This is chiefly the aim of modern historico-critical studies which attempt to delineate either the author's original intention or the various historical contexts underlying each text. This is necessarily psychological in emphasis, since it is based on the interpreter's psychological ability to penetrate the "implied" consciousnesses underlying the texts. Its validity rests on the continuity of the human mind throughout the ages, but its difficulty resides in its aims. Seeking what is only "implied" is possible, but risky and exceedingly difficult to verify. Arguing by "implication" is ultimately never rigidly verifiable.[2] Yet, this is a necessary task, for without it we would have no way of historically reconstructing the texts in question.

Second, besides the analysis of what is "implied" by the text, there is the analysis of the text itself. This is the focus of modern interpretation theory, and builds especially upon the work of Paul Ricoeur and Hans-Georg Gadamer. It is based on the notion that a written text is something qualitatively distinct from either its author's original intentions or its original historical contexts. As Tracy puts it, "Once I write, it is my text alone which bears the meaning, not my intention in writing it, not my original audience's reaction to it."[3] On this view, the meaning of the text is an ideal one, "distanced" from the implied author and contexts, and susceptible of retrieval through semantical, not psychological, methods.

Finally, however, besides the analyses of what is either implied by the text itself or ideally present in the text, there is the meaning which we ourselves give to the text. No amount of study of the text alone will yield this "meaning," for it is supplied by our own imaginative capacities. It is not arbitrary, however, so long as it builds upon the above hermeneutical methods and adequately accounts for their findings. This is the kind of interpretation Freud engaged in when he interpreted cultural history in the light of his theory of the Oedipus complex. The texts alone could not yield this interpretation, for it came from Freud's *own* creative capacities. Freud's mistake came, *not* from his extrapolations from his present self-understanding, but from the inadequacies of the Oedipus complex notion. Similarly, the axial interpretation which we propose to make of the New Testament falls within the ambit of this imaginative hermeneutics. In this kind of hermeneutics, the text serves as a catalyst for our own imaginative capacities.

The method here is neither psychological (penetrating the "implied" consciousnesses of the authors) nor semantical, but imaginative: if the axial theory is valid, it can then illuminate aspects of the New Testament for the contemporary mind. The first two hermeneutical methods are more past-oriented: what does the past either "imply" or "say." This method is more future-oriented: the text is treated as a catalyst for developing and partially confirming present self-understanding.[4]

The Emergence of Individuation in Israel

Any attempt to understand Christ's contribution to the axial period must begin with his Hebraic background, for it is out of this that his contribution emerged. First, I would like to underscore my debt to Eric Voegelin,[5] for to my mind he has most clearly demonstrated the presence of axial consciousness in at least trito-Isaiah and Jeremiah. Thus sometime in the eighth and seventh centuries B.C. we can see the breakthrough to individuality and freedom emerging in Israel. Possibly the transition to city life and thus conventional consciousness is signalized by Abraham's journey from Ur, the intent of which was to establish "a great nation" (cf. Gen. 12:1-3). In any case, the gradual conventionalizing of Israel enables us to understand the extraordinary importance which Israel attached to the "covenant," to the "decalogue," and to "ritual laws," all of which can be seen as means toward the conventionalizing of Israelite life. The transition to conventional life did not take place without a struggle, as the argument over the establishment of a monarchy clearly points out.[6] The establishment of the monarchy, however, did in principle point to Israel's conventionalizing and thus to the increasing development of rational thinking.

The evidence indicates that Israel entered into axial consciousness through its increasingly rational understanding of God. As Cobb puts it: "The clarification and development of human self-understanding was for Hebrew man a function of his beliefs about Yahweh."[7] It is not that Israel first discovered God in the axial period. What we should rather think of is a progressive maturation in its view of the deity, from a primarily mythical (pre-conventional) to a national (conventional), and then finally to a post-conventional understanding of God. Out of this progressive maturation emerged a correspondingly mature understanding of man. What precipitated this rationalized understanding of Yahweh was very likely Israel's own political situation. The conquering of the northern and southern kingdoms of Israel by neighboring powers had forced Israel to reinterpret itself. If its own national God—Yahweh—was still to be understood as the guiding power behind Israel's fate, this Yahweh would have to be understood as the God behind the acts of Israel's neighbors. Thus, it was not rationality itself which directly caused a reinterpretation of Israel's God. I am only maintaining, as we shall see, that this new interpretation presupposed an advanced rational and abstractive ability.

The rationalized understanding of Yahweh is exemplified in the prohibition against images of the deity (Ex. 33:20). What this ultimately required was that the Israelite understand God as neither a tribal deity nor a national deity, each of which was to localize him, but as a transcendent deity, "the God of heaven and the God of earth" (Gen. 24:3). Naturally this kind of conception of the deity could only emerge when man's rational capacities were quite developed, for it presupposed the ability to abstract, to distance oneself from the localizable. It seems that only in Jeremiah and the later Isaiah do we find this notion clearly present:

Before me no god was formed, and after me there shall be none. It is I, I the Lord: there is no savior but me (Is. 43:10-11).

I am the Lord and there is no other, there is no God besides me. It is I who arm you, though you know me not, so that toward the rising and the setting of the sun men may know that there is none besides me. I am the Lord, there is no other; I form the light, and create the darkness, I make well-being and create woe: I, the Lord, do all these things (Is. 45:5-7).

This rationalized understanding of Yahweh fostered a new way of thinking about God. Nature images, fostered by mythical thinking, were no longer viable, and Cobb suggests that "a vague mode of understanding emerged among the Hebrews, which can best be pointed to in our vocabulary by the idea of person."[8]

The implications of a personalized God for the Hebraic understanding of man were profound. Already in the somewhat rationalized phase of the Israel before Jeremiah and the late Isaiah a more personalized view of God and man had developed. The "thou shalt" of the legal codes (Ex. 20—23) implied that the person was capable of responsibility for his own actions, though this was not consistently thought through, as the notion of collective guilt (2 Sam. 21) shows. This latter notion was probably bound up with Israel's sense of "corporate personality," and probably reflected a predominantly conventional consciousness. That is, the individual is accorded worth because he belonged to a community, not because he was an individual as such. Further, capital punishment was not inflicted for crimes against property, which illustrates an emerging sense of the value of personhood. Even slaves were accorded certain rights (Ex. 21). Finally, in this transitional phase, the appeal to the heart manifests an emerging sense of personality: "Take to heart these words which I enjoin on you today" (Dt. 6:6).

We must look, however, to the prophetic movement, and especially to the late prophets, for the consistently personalized understanding of God and man. As Eichrodt understands it, "Most remarkable . . . are the new form and forceful concentration of the relation with God, which had hitherto simply been described as the fear of God, and is now expressed in words like faith, love, thankfulness, and knowledge of God, which are filled with spiritual tension."[9] This personalized view of God brought forth an equally personalized view of man: the individual in the proper sense was emerging. A God who asked for faith, love, thankfulness, and knowledge implied a man capable of giving them. Similarly, it fostered a transvaluation of Israel's legal code, which increasingly became the kind of ethical legislation through which genuine human freedom as we

know it could emerge. The prophetic motto *Shubu!*—Turn!—
implied that man must decide, or, better, that he was a being
capable of decision. The constant critique of the cult—"Not
sacrifice, but obedience" (1 Sam. 15:22; Am. 5:21-24; Hos. 6:6;
Is. 1:1-11; Jer. 7:21-23)—was really a critique of those factors
impeding the emergence of authentic human freedom and responsibility. Again we quote Eichrodt: "The man to whom
God's demand comes is recognized as a person, an I, who
cannot be represented or replaced by any other."[10]

Few scholars have so carefully detailed the prophetic
breakthrough to axial consciousness as Eric Voegelin. Only
Jaspers and Eichrodt come close to the force of Voegelin's
ability to communicate the epochal nature of these events. A
first example from Voegelin is his explanation of the prophets'
problem. The evidence indicates that their primary tool for
reform was the decalogue. It had to be, for only this had been
commonly assimilated by the Israelites. Thus, Jeremiah's great
temple address (Jer. 7) relied upon it, and the prophets in general either at least reflected it or directly quoted from it (Hos.
6:8-10; Mic. 2:1-2, 8-9; Jer. 5:1-6; borrowing from the deca-
logues of Dt. 5 and Ex. 20). But the decalogue itself was their
problem. Emerging from the conventionalized phase of Israel's
existence, its legal form did not allow for a thoroughly personalized and post-conventional understanding of God and
man. The decalogue all too easily fostered that collective and
conventional consciousness which the prophets felt driven to
critique. The prophets, then, had to forge not only a new understanding but a new vocabulary. The misunderstanding this
met with undoubtedly explains Jeremiah's famous exasperation
with his countrymen (Jer. 44).

A further example from Voegelin helps us understand why
we date the axial breakthrough with Jeremiah in the seventh
century B.C. Already we have indicated the gradual nature of
the axial breakthrough, and Voegelin has detailed its gradual
development in the prophets themselves. While the new sense
of individuality and freedom had gone a long way toward maturation in the eighth-century prophets Amos and Hosea, nonetheless Voegelin refers to their contribution as the "institutional phase" of prophetic development. In our terms, while

there is a clear movement toward a post-conventional ethics, Amos and Hosea still conceive Israel's salvation in ultimately conventional terms. Not so much a new self-understanding but a restored society will liberate Israel: "I will bring about the restoration of my people Israel; they shall rebuild and inhabit their ruined cities" (Am. 9:14; cf. Hos. 3:4-5). The fruitlessness of this approach had first to be experienced before a full entry into axial consciousness could emerge. This experience is termed by Voegelin the "metastatic phase," and is exemplified in the early Isaiah (Is. 1—40). While Isaiah flirts with the notion that Israel's salvation will again be a restored society (Is. 7:1-9), he moves to a vision which is increasingly apocalyptic. That is, he seems to give up on any human solution at all, and prefers to simply hope for Yahweh's *ruah* to bring salvation (Is. 11:1-9). Here I would say we have a perception of the breakdown of a simply conventional consciousness, but Isaiah's alternative is equally fruitless. Waiting for Yahweh's spirit simply ushered in approximately one hundred years of prophetic silence which was only broken by later Isaiah (Is. 40—66) and Jeremiah. As Voegelin states it: "The long silence would indicate the sterility of waiting for the metastasis."[11]

According to Voegelin, it is with Jeremiah that we have the breakthrough to a thoroughly axial, post-conventional consciousness:

What is new in his extant work are the pieces of spiritual autobiography, in which the problems of prophetic existence, the concentration of order in the man who speaks the word of God, become articulate. The great motive that had animated the prophetic criticism of conduct and commendation of the virtues had at last been traced to its source in the concern with the order of personal existence under God. In Jeremiah the human personality had broken the compactness of collective existence and recognized itself as the authoritative source of order in society.[12]

Jeremiah no longer waits for a king who will redeem Israel through a restoration of an orderly, conventionalized mode of existence. He transfers the royal symbolism to himself (Jer.

1:10, 18:1-12), thus indicating that full personal individuality and self-responsibility are the hoped-for salvation. This is why Voegelin emphasizes Jeremiah's autobiographical pieces (Jer. 12, 15, 20): they are clear illustrations of his breakthrough to a post-conventional consciousness and individuation. In Jeremiah the individuated and responsible "I" has clearly emerged: "When *I* found your words, *I* devoured them; they became *my* joy and the happiness of *my* heart, because *I* bore your name, O Lord, God of hosts" (Jer. 15:16). Like all breakthroughs, however, it was preceded by a crisis, in which Jeremiah discovered the breakdown of former modes of consciousness. For example, the conspiracy on his life (Jer. 12) was probably typical of the kinds of experiences which forced him to discover his own personality as the "battlefield of existence under Yahweh," to use Voegelin's terms.

So far as we can tell, the extant Old Testament texts were eventually redacted in the light of the later prophetic, axial maturation.[13] Elements of pre-axial phases of consciousness were mingled with axial insights in the final redaction. Despite this difficulty, it is possible to single out the transforming effects that the axial breakthrough had on certain key features of Israelite belief. For example, the matured view of God and man brought with it a new sense of history. In the personalized understanding of a God who calls men to decision and responsibility, "time" took on a new meaning as an unpredictable and open-ended reality: the locus of God's summons: "Therefore I will again deal with this people in surprising and wondrous fashion" (Is. 29:14). In Eichrodt's words: "Time becomes . . . the unrecurring reality which is given by God and which urges man to a decision; the reality which inexorably calls for a decision here and now and permits no rests in some secure position which is valid once for all."[14] It is in this light that we should understand the importance which Israel assigned to certain historical events (viz., the Exodus, Mount Sinai). In the light of an axial consciousness those events were simply intensive experiences highlighting the decisional nature of all of history. This was a way of experiencing history not open to the mythically-oriented person, for a mind that mimes nature is a mind that feels limited to nature's recurrent and cyclical make-up.

Further, I would personally understand the importance which Israel assigned to God as Creator as the result of at least the beginnings of axial consciousness. Contemporary Old Testament scholarship tends to indicate that the creation texts were the result of the redactors and projections back into history's beginnings on the basis of their later, more matured self-understanding. Our own axial interpretation would lend credence to this, insofar as the mythical way of thinking, tied to nature as it was, would have fostered a naturalistic view of the deity. The gods would have been part of the world, and not transcendent to it as is Israel's Creator. The denaturalized and personalized Creator, a conception fostered by axial consciousness, in turn presupposed a more personalized view of man: man is made in God's image (Gen. 1).

The Non-Hebraic Axis: Some Observations
on Greek and Oriental Individuation

From the perspective we are pursuing, what qualifies a breakthrough as "axial" is the emergence of individuality and freedom: the individuated and autonomous "ego." But while this seems to be a characteristic shared by all the axial leaders, the evidence also indicates that there are qualitative differences in the individuation that each promises. In the case of Israel, individuation emerges as a result of its matured understanding of Yahweh. Like Voegelin, I prefer to qualify this as a "pneumatic differentiation," since it seems to introduce into human consciousness an awareness of being called or chosen, which we traditionally refer to as "grace." From the perspective of human development, it is a matter of no small interest that the perception of reality as a grace seems to emerge in Israel. For the moment we should at least notice that this would require a very advanced degree of individuation. In a pre-conventional phase of existence, the awareness of oneself as "grace" or "specially chosen" must be lacking, simply because there is no clear awareness of the self-as-worthy-of-love. In a conventionalized ambience, the self has still not differentiated itself sufficiently to grasp itself as an object of love on its own account. It is the conventions of society that still define the worth of the individual, not vice versa. Personally, this is how I would understand Israel's sense of "corporate personality," made so famous by H. Wheeler Robinson. It is only where individuation has decisively broken through into human consciousness and thus in a post-conventional phase that the individual can perceive himself as an object of love or grace on his own account. It is in this light that I would personally understand the need for a "new covenant," so emphasized in Jeremiah. The "old" covenant, primarily the result of Israel's conventionalized phase of existence, simply was inadequate to the new level of consciousness attained by the highly individuated Jeremiah. Jeremiah's new covenant of the heart (Jer. 31:33) is simply his expression of an individuality that knows itself to be absolutely loved. I think the important matter to underline at this point is that this discovery emerged in Israel only because it entered into axial consciousness primarily as a result of its reflection upon God. I think it safe to say that the other, non-Hebraic, axial leaders took different routes, and this because the focus of their maturation was precisely not in reflection upon God.

As Cobb especially underlines, Israel entered into axial consciousness through its increasingly rational reflection upon Yahweh. Its focus was Yahweh, and rationality developed in function of that. It never focused simply upon reason for its own sake. It was in Greece that rationality emerged as the clear focus of attention, and while this was Greece's greatness, I also want to indicate that it hindered the development of an awareness of the "gracious nature" of reality, with all that such an awareness implies.

The evidence indicates that the Greeks entered into axial consciousness through their rational critique of Olympian religion, especially as evidenced in the work of Homer.[15] What Homer did was to "treat the myths as if they were the bearers of intelligible meanings. . . . In this way arose the mythological in distinction from the mythical."[16] Implied in this move, of course, was a heightened sense of one's rational abilities. As Richardson puts it:

[It presupposed] man's capacity to withhold himself from action in order to contemplate and simply view. Today we call man's capacity to purge himself of passions and volitions in order to contemplate something "objectively" man's reason; man's reason is his capacity . . . to know in a theoretical, or purely contemplative way.[17]

I would maintain that it was this contemplative or abstractive ability that came to the fore in Greece and that explains why philosophy was able to make the gains that it did in Greece. Socrates, perhaps, immortalized what this discovery must have meant to the Greeks when he identified himself with reason itself. In Socrates we can see how the Greek discovery of reason had come to displace all else in man's makeup: the Socratic ideal is the man whose total existence is dominated by reason. But while this was the greatness of the Greeks, it was also their problem. For reason had its limits, as the Greek conception *moira* or *fate* itself indicated. While the history of the Greek notion of *moira* is an extremely complex one, I would only suggest that it witnesses to the ultimate inadequacy of reducing man simply to reason. The Greeks had to find some way to account for the irrational, and *moira* witnesses to their attempt to do so.

At this point, I think, we can underline a key difference between the Grecian and the Hebraic entries into axial consciousness. In the Hebraic view, life was governed by Yahweh, a personalized God who summoned man to a personalized modality of existence. This tended to foster the conditions in which full individuality and responsibility could develop. A life governed by fate ultimately inhibited a developed sense of responsibility, for the latter can only prosper where there exists a sense that one really does have control over one's existence. Fate implies that one ultimately has no control. Cobb's insight is crucial here:

In their brilliant ethical reflections, the Greeks always explained failure to do the good in such a way that from our point of view no real responsibility therefore can be attributed to the wrongdoer. The clear emergence of responsible personhood . . . occurred only in Israel.[18]

Greece, then, seems to have entered into rational consciousness directly through its increased ability to rationalize. In the Orient, too, of Hinduism, Buddhism and Taoism, the evidence suggests that an entry into axial consciousness emerged, again, through the heightening of one's rational capacities. But whereas in Greece rationality was thought to be a positive value in itself, and thus to be developed and enhanced, in the Orient a different route (or routes) was pursued. Rationality, we have often said, presupposes a sense of individuation, insofar as it presupposes an "I" capable of distancing itself from external reality. But rationality can variously be responded to. In Greece, it was seen as primarily "good" and its continued development enhanced one's sense of individuation. For the Greeks, reason was a power to be developed; in the Orient, it was a power to be critiqued. A heightened sense of individuality, after all, can foster a heightened sense of aloneness and estrangement. Cobb suggests, for example, that this was the way the Buddhist primarily experienced reason. And this led the Buddhist not to reject reason and individuality but to render them ineffectual through altered states of consciousness. The fruits of reason and individuality—inquisitiveness, analysis, dissection, alienated sense of self—are replaced by serenity, disinterestedness, and perfect unconcern. Schwartz seems to give a similar interpretation to Taoism.[19] To my mind, this approach to the human problem—we can call it the mystical approach—represents a very great degree of individuation, insofar as it would demand a very secure and individuated ego not to desire even desire. And further, it is not in its "mystical" emphasis that I would see the difference between Oriental wisdom and the developments flowing from the Jewish axis. Mystical elements present in both Judaism and Christianity would seem to argue for a certain compatibility between the Oriental and Jewish axes. Rather I would ask whether rendering the fruit of individuation ineffectual is a sufficient answer to the human problem. In the Jewish axis, as we shall see, the answer was sought more directly from God than from man's own ability to alter his consciousness.

To my mind, just why the Oriental axis experienced its entrance into axial rationality skeptically remains a puzzling question. At this stage of my own reflections I would offer two observations. First, as we shall see later, the sense of alienation was already an issue in the Orient, owing to the ancient doctrine of transmigration, which seemed to offer no path of final escape from the burdens of existence. The heightened axial sense of awareness possibly then accentuated this sense of alienation and seemed to increase the burden of existence. Thus, rationality was an ambiguous reality to be greeted with skepticism. Second, this skeptical view of rationality possibly inhibited the kind of rationalized and personalized view of transcendent reality that occurred in Israel. Notions of the transcendent did, of course, appear in the Orient, but it would seem that Buddha's skepticism about rationally penetrating the nature of the transcendent reflects the more common Oriental approach to the transcendent.

Christ and the Emergence of Christian Individuation

Are we permitted to speak of a new level of consciousness initiated by Jesus and coming into existence with the first Christian community? The scholar who has devoted the most attention to this question, John Cobb, thinks so: "My interest lies in the actual and effective emergence of a new structure of existence, and as a matter of historical fact, this occurred only by the total impact of Jesus' transformation of Jewish teaching combined with his resurrection appearances."[20] I will rely greatly on Cobb's views here, although I will differ with him somewhat. Instead of speaking of Jesus' transformation of Jewish teaching, I would prefer to speak of a renewal, an intensification, and even a radicalizing. I do not think we can speak of a transformation, and thus the breakthrough to a new level of individuated consciousness, until the resurrection event itself. I would suggest that the resurrection belief witnesses to a transformation of the Christian community itself, initiating a new level of consciousness, insofar as the risen one became—as risen—a new basis from which to understand human destiny. Throughout we have spoken of the gradual nature of the axial breakthroughs, and I think the evidence forces us to maintain this gradualist approach in our view of Jesus. The pre-Easter Jesus, insofar as we can retrieve him through historical reconstruction,[21] witnesses to the gradual intensification of Hebraic consciousness in Jesus himself, an intensification which prepared the way for a new "resurrectional" differentiation of consciousness.

Let us begin with Cobb's analysis of the pre-Easter Jesus, an analysis which contemporary biblical hermeneutics would seem to confirm. First, Jesus renewed the prophetic experience of the present immediacy of God. We can only speculate as to why this prophetic experience had been lost. Partly, I would suggest, it was due to the pre-axial development of the Israelites. Axial consciousness appeared only in *some* of the prophets, and, as we earlier pointed out, such minorities take a great deal of time to succeed. The Pharisees, who were the normative Jewish party of Jesus' time, seem to represent a mixture of pre-axial and axial (prophetic) elements. The normative status of this party can be taken as an indication that either the Israelites generally had only incompletely attained axial consciousness, or that, once attained, it had been lost. Cobb suggests that the problem was partly due to the prophets themselves. Involved in the prophetic rationalizing of Yahweh was a distancing of the divine, which we earlier termed the awareness of the transcendent as such. For the prophets themselves, this was not a loss of God's immediacy, but a transformation in their experience of it. The former "numinous" immediacy fostered by mythical thinking had become a "personalized" immediacy. But a personalized immediacy is not a concrete, tangible, and naturalistic immediacy, the only "immediacy" pre-axial people knew. Hence, the loss of divine immediacy on the part of large numbers: God's "actual present effectiveness became a matter of belief rather than of immediate apprehension."[22] In this light, we can perhaps understand the people's constant desire, evidenced in the prophetic literature, to return to polytheism. In part, of course, this was a desire to relapse back into a pre-axial state, which was intelligible enough when we grasp the personal demands that axial consciousness makes. In part, however, it was the expression of an authentic spiritual desire to recapture the divine immediacy fostered by mythical thinking.

Nonetheless, in Jesus we find the Hebraic ethically responsible individual—which Pharisaism had not lost—and the intense experience of God's immediacy, simultaneously. It is in this light that we should understand the findings of contemporary historical and textual-semantical scholarship.[23] Both point to a divine immediacy in Jesus which manifests an intensification of the prophetic experience of divine immediacy. Jeremias' studies on Jesus' use of "Abba" is one example that could be pointed to. Similarly, we could point to David Tracy's analysis of New Testament language as a limit-language fostering an immediate sense of God's presence. Cobb concentrates on Jesus' proclamation of the imminence of the Kingdom. According to Cobb, Jesus' sense of the Kingdom did not stem from a sense of God's absence. This was the view of apocalypticism within mainstream Judaism. Hence, for them, the Kingdom is not "now," but only expected. Jesus' sense of divine immediacy, however, resulted in a present experience of the Kingdom. Once we understand the intensity of Jesus' experience, we need not take too literally and exclusivistically the current biblical debate as to whether Jesus preached a wholly present Kingdom or one yet to be completed in the future. As James Mackey perceptibly puts it: "No man who has the kind of faith in God the Father which Jesus had could be without the firm expectation that God would work to rectify the wrongs of the world, nor would he be without the strongest hope that God would sustain and enrich himself and his fellows in a creative act that could overcome even the tragedy of death."[24]

Cobb's second point is that Jesus completed what the prophets set out to do by freeing the prophetic ethical teaching from archaic, pre-axial elements. Given Pharisaism's interpretation of the prophetic ethics, we must say that the prophets initiated Israel's entry in axial consciousness; Jesus, in principle, completed it. Among the pre-axial elements which Jesus critiqued, Pharisaic casuistry must be mentioned as witnessing to an incomplete axial consciousness. It did not clearly distinguish between genuine ethical principles flowing from the priority of individual human worth, and ancient taboos and cultic laws reminiscent of a "conventionalized" consciousness. Further, this same conventionalized consciousness showed up in the way the Pharisees interpreted the supreme commandment of love. This latter they interpreted in the context of the law (legal "conventions"), whereas for Jesus the law was thoroughly rationalized by the axial emphasis on love. Here we see a radicalization of Jeremiah's new covenant of the heart. Finally, the prophetic God-centeredness reached a new pitch in Jesus, insofar as ethical demands were thought to flow, not from human, casuistic calculation, but from God's present summons to man.

Finally, according to Cobb, Jesus radicalized the prophetic trust in God. This both recaptured and intensified the experience of freedom so exemplified in the prophets. As we have seen, the prophetic experience of Yahweh issued forth in an intense personal freedom, insofar as the personalized Yahweh summoned the individual to an equally personalized mode of existence. When the prophets thought that Israel's legal code inhibited this personalization, they were led to critique it. The Pharisees only incompletely understood this, as their interpretation of the supreme command to love in the context of justice manifested. Pharisaic freedom was a freedom to fulfill the prescriptions of the law. Jesus' freedom was one which could lead even beyond the law.

From my perspective, what all of this evidence witnesses to is the gradual nature of human development, a thesis we have sought to defend throughout our analyses in this essay. As we can point to an intensification of elements previously present in former phases of development, prior to every breakthrough, I see no reason why we cannot make the same application in the case of Jesus. All of this evidence indicates, then, that Jesus radicalized the Hebraic entry into axial consciousness. The resurrection itself, however, precipitated an awareness of the final meaning of this radicalization and thus initiated a qualitatively new level of consciousness within the axial period.

Before turning to the resurrection, however, something needs to be said about the critical importance of Jesus' death by crucifixion. If Jesus' life and ministry can properly be said to have radicalized the Hebraic entry into axial consciousness, Jesus' death glaringly sums up what such a consciousness entails, and forever manifests that the style of life characteristic of radical God-centeredness is not the negation of this-worldly responsibility, but its intensification to the furthest limits. The suffering and death of Jesus were a radical manifestation that faith in God liberates the individual to accept the full implications of his freedom and responsibility. Here again we find that peculiar combination of the intense experience of God's immediacy and the ethically responsible individual, which in the Hebrew Scriptures was indicated by the "suffering servant" and now in Jesus' death is renewed. Perhaps most vividly in the cross can we glimpse that Jesus means to free mankind from all pre-axial elements, for the "good life" is now no longer indicated by fidelity to taboos and legal prescriptions, but only in selfless responsibility and freedom, even the freedom to die. But now we must turn to the resurrection, for it is this that removed any barrier in the way of properly deciphering the true meaning of Jesus' life, ministry, and death.

In speaking of the resurrection, and in placing the emphasis that I do upon it, I realize that I am entering into a much disputed terrain of biblical and theological inquiry. Nonetheless, I am convinced that Christianity is unintelligible without it. Further, I am convinced that our axial interpretation of Jesus throws a new light upon the subject. As I have approached our subject consistently from the point of view of the development of human consciousness, I will do the same with the resurrection. Instead of concentrating on the facticity[25] of the resurrection, as much contemporary scholarship does, I will ask, rather, what quality of consciousness and individuation the resurrection belief presupposes and makes possible. This neither solves nor denies the factual question, although from our developmental perspective consciousness always develops from an interaction with experience itself. The attempt to reduce the resurrection simply to a subjective creation of the early Church does some justice to the subjective pole of human development, but it ignores or does inadequate justice to the objective or experimental pole.[26]

First, it should be clear that the evidence attests that the resurrection is a theory or belief of the first Christians. None of the Gospels describe the event itself, and there are no recorded witnesses to it. What the evidence witnesses to are the appearances, and the resurrection belief can be taken as the attempt on the disciples' part to decipher the meaning of those appearances. The scholarly inability to reconcile the appearance accounts in the Gospels and in Paul, the alternate interpretation of the event as an "exaltation" or "ascension" of Christ, the later tendency of the biblical tradition to unite the resurrection and exaltation traditions—all of this points to the fact that we are dealing with a theory (or theories) grappling with what has occurred in Jesus. From this perspective, then, we are justified in treating the resurrection as a belief, and indeed as the dominant interpretation of what occurred in Jesus. For us, the key issue is: What quality of consciousness does such a belief entail?

Thus far, no satisfying explanation of the resurrection itself has won a complete acceptance among theologians.[27] Despite this fact, there is no doubt, among Christians at any rate, that it transformed the early Christian disciples. On the one hand, Jesus' resurrection led to the conviction that death itself had not ended Jesus' relationship with his disciples (Lk. 24:1-53). On the other hand, if we seek to translate this conviction into the terms of human consciousness, we find that it manifests a new development of man's consciousness.[28] For what such a conviction presupposed was a heightened perception of a transcendent source of personal identity, a source which was now clearly known to transcend mutability, decay, and even death. As Herbert Richardson put it, what emerged in consciousness was the following understanding:

There was a higher kind of life above and beyond the life of nature and history. There was a Life that was not subject to mutability and death and decay, a Life whose structure and order pervaded every biological and historical entity and caused them to be alive.[29]

Now the self had become radically aware of its spiritual and transcendent nature. It knew that it was more than simply physical or biological, and thus capable of transcending the elements of decay and even death. From this point of view, the resurrection belief completed the Hebraic entry into axial consciousness by revealing the last implications of belief in a transcendent God. What we must imagine here is man's gradual discovery of his own transcendent and spiritual nature. The prophetic discovery of a transcendent God fostered the emergence of a personalized and spiritualized understanding of man. The prophet thus knew himself as a spiritual self, more than simply physical or biological. But this was a spiritual self in its beginnings, not yet sure of its own radically spiritual and transcendent nature. The resurrection belief removed every barrier in the way of understanding the thoroughly spiritual nature of the self. To believe in the resurrection presupposed a radically spiritual and transcendent view of selfhood.[30] I am not maintaining, of course, that it was only in Christianity that belief in the resurrection emerged. Various forms of a collective resurrection belief existed in Israel and elsewhere, as we know.[31] As O'Collins correctly indicates: "In the faith of Israel belief in resurrection emerged as a corollary of theism."[32] The gradual emergence of resurrection beliefs points to the gradual emergence of an increasingly spiritual and transcendent view of selfhood. However, I would maintain that Jesus' ministry and resurrection brought this process of man's spiritualization to its completion and removed every barrier to its complete emergence.

From the point of view of the history of human consciousness it is a further question whether we accept the truth-value of this discovery. What is rather important for our purposes is the quality of consciousness which this belief generated. While I think that the differences between Judaism and Christianity can be exaggerated, I do think there is merit in the notion of a qualitative difference between the two. In brief, the more radicalized understanding of divine transcendence implied by the resurrection belief generated a more radicalized form of individuated consciousness among the early Christian disciples. For one thing, the heightened awareness of divine transcendence, as a force transcending and permeating all things finite and subject to decay, generated a heightened awareness of the divine initiative and presence in the Christian's psyche. In Cobb's words, "God was known as empowering presence at least as clearly as he was known as heavenly Father."[33] But, simultaneously, this heightened sense of the divine initiative and presence equally heightened the breakthrough to individuation and personal responsibility that characterized the Hebraic entry into axial consciousness. Of course, the heightened awareness of the divine initiative could—and, as we shall see, did at times—collapse the awareness of personal individuation and self-responsibility. When this occurred, we could speak of a regression to a pre-axial and pre-individuated phase of existence. But, in normative Christianity at least, the Hebraic axial individuation was enhanced and accentuated. If we take the elements of self-responsibility and freedom as the chief characteristics of Hebraic axial consciousness, we find that both these elements have been accentuated in normative Christianity. The ultimate enemy of self-responsibility is fatalism. The individual cannot regard himself as responsible for elements which are not susceptible of any kind of control. The heightened awareness of the divine presence, as a power enabling the individual to transcend all forces of decay and even death itself, removed the obstacle of fatalism from the Christian consciousness. The Christian found himself capable of responsibly confronting every obstacle to human existence. Somehow the empowering presence of God activated and heightened his own self-responsibility. Paul, for example, found himself capable of confronting every imaginable obstacle: death, life, the powers of the cosmos, present and future, and every living creature (Rom. 8:35-39).

The counterpart to a heightened self-responsibility was a heightened freedom. At this point, I cannot resist quoting Cobb:

Man was free from the law, because he could live immediately from the grace that was the Spirit. He did not need to struggle to obey imposed principles of conduct, because his heart was changed. Those principles were now either set aside as irrelevant or accepted as the spontaneous expression of the new heart that he found within himself as the work of the Spirit. Man was free from his own past, because the Spirit placed him on a new level of existence in which that past had no power over him. Man was free from the oppressive powers of this world, the structures within the context of which he had understood his existence, because he now lived in terms of a reality that radically transcended and rationalized them.[34]

Cobb hits on the essential element that came into focus in the Christian consciousness as a result of the resurrection: "He now lived in terms of a reality that radically transcended and rationalized [the oppressive powers of this world]." The New Testament itself, as the first and thus most primitive attempt to explain this experience, variously referred to this "reality" as God (Yahweh), the risen Jesus, and the Spirit. The "Spirit"-terminology was perhaps most apt for expressing this heightened awareness of the empowering divine presence, a factor which undoubtedly accounts for its frequency in the New Testament. But since we are focusing on the emergence of the quality of consciousness, this conflict in terminology is not really decisive. What is more important for this essay is the need to somehow characterize the kind of human consciousness which emerged in Christianity.

We have sought all along to maintain that what characterized a consciousness as "axial" was its character as "individuated," its consciousness of being a self-responsible and autonomous individual. To various degrees, all the axial leaders manifested the characteristics of this individuated consciousness. With the emergence of individuation, those factors which impeded the development of responsibility and autonomous freedom also emerged as key problems. The counterpart to the process of the individuation of the personality was the danger of the disintegration of that same personality. Greece attempted to deal with the possible disintegration of the personality through reason, and the eventual immortalizing of "reason" can be taken as Greece's attempt to show that complete human individuation could be attained and that all factors threatening the individual could be overcome. Greece's answer to the problem and possibility of individuation was to be found in man's own rational consciousness itself. The Oriental axis, to the extent that I understand it, sought the answer in man's own consciousness also. The very reality which heightened one's awareness of the threat to individuation—rational consciousness—was to be relativized through altered states of consciousness. The Jewish axis came at the problem differently. The prophet defined himself in terms of a transcendent source of identity. The prophet knew himself to be an "I" because God was understood to be the great "Thou." Likewise, the prophet sought the answer to the forces that threaten to disintegrate the personality in this same transcendent source. The same God that granted man a real personality would enable him to achieve his destiny. Israel thus sought the answer to individuation not in man himself, but in God. Now it was this same belief in a transcendent source of identity which was further accentuated in Christianity. As a result of the resurrection, the Christian believed that every force which threatens to disintegrate the individual personality had been relativized. Every obstacle to individuation was thought to be removed. Mircea Eliade brings home well what this meant:

> If Abraham's faith can be defined as "for God everything is possible," the faith of Christianity implies that everything is also possible for man. "Have faith in God. For verily I say unto you, that whosoever shall say unto this mountain, Be thou removed, and be thou cast into the sea; and shall not doubt in his heart, but shall believe that those things which he saith shall come to pass, he shall have whatsoever he saith. Therefore I say unto you, what things soever ye desire, when ye pray, believe that ye receive them, and ye shall have them" (Mk. 11:22-24). Faith, in this context, as in many others, means absolute emancipation from any kind of natural "law" and hence the highest freedom that man can imagine: freedom to intervene even in the ontological constitution of the universe. It is, consequently, a pre-eminently creative freedom.[35]

The resurrection belief rightly conjures up in the human imagination the image of the fulfilled man who has conquered all forces threatening to destroy human individuation. That this belief became the central belief in Christianity argues for the emergence in Christianity of a psyche that believed itself capable of full human individuation. Such a psyche could not have emerged unless it experienced the presence of a transcendent spiritual source, co-constituting its very self, empowering it to transcend all forces threatening to destroy the self.

At this point I would like to emphasize my debt to Erich Neumann's own analysis of the evolution of human consciousness. My own interpretation of the quality of consciousness implied by the resurrection belief was greatly stimulated by Neumann's superb analysis of the many resurrection myths which have appeared in man's history. Briefly put, Neumann believes that there is an evolution in man's myth-making, and that the various developments in myth reflect, in projected form, man's own development in consciousness. He considers the resurrection myths to be the sediments of man's latest phase of development, namely, the emergence of individuation. In Neumann's account, the fully individuated ego emerges when it is sufficiently consolidated and stabilized so as to counteract the danger of disintegration, and thus to resist regression to a pre-individuated phase of existence. The resurrection myths, then, are the mythological prototypes of the ego's attainment of stability and indestructibility, of the conquest of death and of the emergence of man's capacity to defend itself against death's power, "for death is the primordial symbol of the decay and dissolution of the personality."[36] As he puts it, "With Osiris . . . resurrection means realizing his eternal and lasting essence, becoming a perfected soul, escaping from the flux of natural occurrence."[37] The resurrection myth, then, projects man's own attainment of individuation, for it presupposes an individuated psyche, a fully formed and consolidated ego, an ego which has differentiated itself from the flux of natural occurrence and decay. For this kind of myth to occur, the self must experience itself as more than simply natural or biological; it must be a "spiritual" self, capable of transcending the natural and biological. We see in the resurrection myths "the visible emergence of the spiritual principle from the natural or biological principle . . . where the accent falls on spirit."[38]

Neumann's influence on my own interpretation of the Christian resurrection belief should be apparent. Like Neumann, I maintain that the Christian resurrection belief presupposes the emergence of a self which is spiritual and that knows itself to be more than simply biological and natural and capable of transcending the elements of decay and death implied in the natural. Unlike Neumann, of course, I maintain that the prophetic discovery of a transcendent God fostered the emergence of this spiritual or transcendent self, and that the Christian resurrection belief fostered the full and complete emergence of such a self. But this difference in interpretation is to be expected, since I am dealing specifically with Judaeo-Christianity. Furthermore, as far as Neumann goes, I have no difficulty with his analysis. But now we come to the heart of the matter. I personally believe that in the later phases of man's mythical period an individuated ego begins to emerge. But what Neumann does not explain is why such a differentiated self emerges. As I have tried to show, it was due to the increasing role that rationality came to play in the great civilizations. Now it is that same individuated ego that Neumann sees "projected" in the resurrection myths that breaks the power of mythical thinking and its projective mode of awareness in the axial period. The overcoming of mythical projection, which largely characterizes the axial period, points to an even greater degree of individuation. An ego which does not project, but subjects reality to its own rational critique, is a vastly more differentiated and individuated ego. Furthermore, by extending our own analysis into the axial period, we are more able than Neumann to carefully distinguish the qualities of individuated consciousness that have emerged in man's history. In Greece, individuated consciousness primarily takes the form of rational consciousness, as we have seen. Such a rational consciousness is a spiritual or transcendent self, which knows itself to be more than simply biological or natural, but its capacity for transcendence is limited by reason. In the Judaeo-Christian axis, however, individuation is a function of belief in an absolutely transcendent God. I would maintain that this leads to a more radically transcendent self, for the Judaeo-Christian capacity for transcendence is not limited simply to reason, but is irrevocably tied to an absolutely transcendent source of identity. The spiritual self of Judaeo-Christianity is a self co-constituted by an empowering divine self.

Our interpretation of the resurrection belief, then, maintains that such a belief fostered the conditions in which full self-responsibility and individuation could develop. As such, it was an axial phenomenon and required a developed axial consciousness to be appropriated. While this was its strength, it was also its weakness. For when an "axial insight" met with a pre-axial consciousness, distortion was bound to occur. The biblical texts themselves indicate that such a distortion had already occurred in Paul's time, and a brief handling of this episode will afford us the opportunity to further clarify the meaning of our "resurrectional consciousness."

The episode to which we refer can be found in Paul's letters to the Corinthians.[39] What we basically find here is a faulty (read: pre-axial) resurrection belief, and thus a faulty or incomplete human individuation. Paul begins by praising the Corinthians, "richly endowed with every gift of speech and knowledge" (1 Cor. 1:5). But a shift occurs, witnessing to Paul's dissatisfaction: "Brothers, the trouble was that I could not talk to you as spiritual men but only as men of flesh, as infants in Christ" (1 Cor. 3:1). And Paul then gets to the heart of his message: "I handed on to you . . . what I myself received, that Christ died for our sins . . . that he was buried and . . . rose on the third day" (1 Cor. 15:3-4). What we notice in Paul is the constant emphasis upon Christ's death; the resurrection is mentioned in conjunction with the death. Early in his first letter Paul makes his emphasis clear: "I determined that while I was with you I would speak of nothing but Jesus Christ and him crucified" (1 Cor. 2:2).

According to Käsemann, what accounts for Paul's emphasis upon the crucified Jesus is the exaggerated and enthusiastic view of the resurrection held by the Corinthians. Evidently they understood the resurrection as the annulment of human responsibility. How else account for the party strife, the exclusion of the deprived from the agapes, the drunken orgies? Because the Corinthians understood the resurrection belief as canceling human responsibility and obedience, they could even say "Cursed be Jesus" (1 Cor. 12:3), meaning by this the pre-Easter suffering Jesus. Paul was thus correcting their resurrection belief. By emphasizing Christ's death, he was trying to show that the responsibility and obedience of Jesus is precisely what the resurrection belief should lead to. The new resurrection consciousness did not annul the cross, whether of Jesus or of the Corinthians. Rather it provided a new standpoint from which the cross could be met. Resurrection belief and individuated responsibility belonged together for Paul. This Corinthian view, critiqued by Paul, is a good example of a relapse into a pre-axial mode of existence. A pre-axial consciousness exists whenever self-responsibility is somehow blocked or fled from.[40] Paul's correction of the enthusiasts' resurrection belief was, then, really an attempt to block a reversion to an archaic level of self-understanding. The deepened Christian awareness of the divine initiative could reduce the Christian to a merely passive instrument of the divine. Were this to occur, the individual would regress to a pre-individuated phase of existence in which the burden and task of self-responsibility is exchanged for the protective and all-embracing care of God. The Church in its later history would call this "quietism" and correctly condemn it. By conjoining the suffering Jesus with the risen Jesus, Paul was attempting to say that the resurrection meant that the divine initiative had been most operative precisely in the life of commitment, service, self-sacrifice and self-responsibility of Jesus. The resurrection, then, was not an annulment of the highly individuated existence which the ministry of Jesus manifested, but rather the confirmation that such a life was precisely what belief in God should lead to.

Resurrectional Consciousness,
"Evolution," and Human Development

Throughout my analysis in this essay I have tried to maintain that development in human consciousness is neither irreversible nor inevitable. The element of reversibility manifests itself in the constant relapses to prior phases of development. The lack of inevitability shows up in those peoples and cultures that have not entered into axial consciousness. For this reason I prefer the term "development" to "evolution." One of the main reasons that Teilhard de Chardin's vision of the Christ meets with such opposition is that he chose the evolutionary model for his own analyses.[41] Teilhard's view, like most classical evolutionary views, tends to have an inevitability about it. This inevitability offends secularists, because it does not adequately account for human freedom, with its sometimes unexpected alterations of the evolutionary process, and for human evil. On the other hand, his views offend religionists, because they seem to compromise divine gratuity, and thus the possibility of the radically new in history. Process philosophers are fond of seeing in God the "principle of novelty," and perhaps the religious unease with Teilhard is an authentic desire to preserve this possibility of novelty in history.

In any case, what I wish to underline here is that our explanation of resurrectional consciousness is meant to be understood within a developmental, not an evolutionary, context. From the point of view of the Hebraic and Christian differentiation, human freedom and divine initiative always belong together. Just as the Hebraic belief in Yahweh's supremacy fostered human freedom and responsibility, so the resurrectional consciousness, rather than annulling human freedom, fosters it. Indeed, the question can be raised whether a genuine human freedom, and thus the possibility of the really new, is possible at all without the Hebraic and Christian view of God. A discussion of this subject would carry us into the metaphysical questions implied by our analysis, and thus beyond the limits of our study.[42] I only desire to point out that it is possible to give an explanation of the Christian consciousness which accords with our more general developmental perspective.

Continuity and Discontinuity

It is obvious that our interpretation of the emergence of Christian consciousness respects another more general developmental principle—namely that every breakthrough, despite the way it appears psychologically to those in whom it occurs, contains elements of continuity and discontinuity. The element of continuity is clear: the resurrectional consciousness is unintelligible without the Hebraic entry into axial consciousness. The individuation resulting from belief in Yahweh is intensified in the Christian consciousness, not annulled. I am, of course, not maintaining that the intensification occurring in Christianity is the only possible direction open to the Hebraic tradition. Later Jewish history, in some respects—for example, Hasidism—has moved in the mystical direction. And, of course, there is the more philosophical and political development of axial consciousness in Enlightenment Judaism and Zionism.

Further, the element of discontinuity is also clear. The biblical texts themselves witness to this. For although Judaism shared in common with Christianity a general resurrection belief (Acts 23:8), still normative Pharisaic Judaism rejected the radical conclusions that Christianity drew from it. Perhaps this also explains why Jesus' own disciples were slow to understand (Mk. 8:32; 9:32). In any case, this element of discontinuity points to the new level of consciousness and mode of existence operative in at least some of the disciples. Perhaps because, as we have indicated, the Christian form of the resurrection belief was not present in Judaism, it was experienced by the first Christians as *radically* new.

It seems to me that several factors need to be kept in mind in our attempt to understand this element of discontinuity. There is a discontinuity that flows from a fundamental incompatibility in orientation. It is historically clear that normative Pharisaic Judaism and many Christians regarded this to be the case. Still, the fact that some pious and believing Jews accepted Christianity argues against a fundamental incompatibility. From a more theoretical viewpoint, if our thesis that Christian consciousness represents an intensification of Hebraic axial consciousness bears merit, then a fundamental incompatibility cannot exist.[43] However, there is a discontinuity that results from a lack of a sufficiently differentiated consciousness. One earlier example of this was the conflict between the prophets, with their developed axial consciousness, and their fellow coun-

trymen, with their predominantly conventional consciousness.
A further example was the conflict between Jesus and Pharisaism. Perhaps we can account for much of the conflict between Christianity and Judaism on the basis of pre-axial mentalities present in both camps, then and now. However, this is a
subject to which we will return in a later chapter of this book,
where we will deal not only with the relationship between Judaism and Christianity, but with other inter-religious relationships as well.

Sublationary, Not Linear

Finally, we can usefully point out that our interpretation
of Christian consciousness accords with our final developmental principle—namely that development is "sublationary"
or a process of complexification, in which previous phases of
development are not simply left behind but continue to manifest themselves in a transformed way. Just as the prophets did
not annul the gains of Israel's conventional phase of existence
(viz., the law, the covenant, the decalogue) but gave them a
new standpoint from which to be understood, so a similar process seems to have occurred in the Christian community.

The first element to be transformed has been well explicat-
ed by Cobb, and we can do little more than present his insights,
though from our somewhat different developmental perspective. He points to the development of a new terminology in
Christianity, emphasizing the role of the Holy Spirit and the
gifts flowing from that Spirit (1 Cor. 12; Jn. 16, etc.).[44] What
Cobb sees here is a recapturing of the mythical experience of
divine immediacy, or an outbreak of the numinous experience
of reality fostered by the more participatory consciousness of a
pre-conventional phase of existence. This is not without its
dangers, for it could lead to a relapse to a more archaic phase
of existence. Being under the Spirit's influence could inhibit
personal responsibility and lead to a sort of infantilism. The
prophets knew this, and thus spoke very little of the Spirit.
Paul knew this too, as his struggle with the Corinthians shows.
Nonetheless, as Cobb indicates, mainstream Christianity did

experience a new outbreak of the Spirit, but it was a spiritual experience transformed by the axial resurrectional consciousness. In Cobb's words:

> Despite the dangers of reversion to archaic existence given with the new prominence of the experience of the Spirit . . . the Church attained an understanding of the work of the Holy Spirit in which the Hebrew axial achievement was affirmed and carried further. Paul . . . saw the essential and characteristic fruit of the presence of the Holy Spirit not in ecstatic phenomena but in a transformation of the quality of the reflective consciousness itself. He saw in the Spirit a pervasive power working continually within the Christian to produce peace, joy, patience, humility, and love.[45]

In our perspective, every reason exists for accepting Cobb's analysis. Christian resurrectional consciousness both restored and transformed the sense of divine immediacy fostered by mythical consciousness. Restored, insofar as God's presence was felt to be an effective one now enabling the person to transcend every human incapacity. Transformed, because this did not annul human responsibility but enhanced the conditions in which it could properly flourish.

A second and final element to which we should call attention is the new sense of community generated by resurrectional consciousness. As our first element above witnesses to a restoration and transformation of a pre-conventional consciousness, so this second element witnesses to the same for a conventional consciousness. As we have seen, the "conventional phase" is characterized by a social sense in which societal conventions both widen the person's consciousness and define his values and goals. The Hebraic covenant is a classic example of this. What we find after the resurrection is a restoration of this social (or conventional) sense. Again, the Scriptures refer to this only in random and *ad hoc* ways, since they could not give the kind of analysis we are engaged in. Luke's Gospel perhaps points to this in a somewhat oblique manner: the risen one is known in the breaking of the bread (Lk. 24:35)—that is, in an experience of community sharing—and he interprets the Scriptures for them (Lk. 24:32)—that is, he gives a new meaning to their community history. However, there are more direct references to a new sense of community.[46] In Paul we find frequent references to a Church as Christ's body and as Christ's continuing presence. In the Gospels we find a missionary command and a commissioning of disciples. This, too, was not without its dangers, for it could signal a relapse into the more archaic, conventionalized mode of existence. This is personally how I would understand Paul's struggles with the Christian "Judaizers."[47] The latter, in attempting to impose the Mosaic prescriptions on all Christians, were really attempting to return to the former conventional mode of existence in which a person's worth is measured by his conformity to societal conventions. Nonetheless, Paul's victory at the Jerusalem council symbolizes the fact that this new sense of community was not only restored but transformed. Resurrectional consciousness gave the disciples a new framework from which to understand the meaning of community. Resurrectional responsibility meant that community was henceforth to be seen primarily as service of the brethren (1 Cor. 12). A person's worth was no longer to be measured by his conformity to societal conventions. Rather, those conventions were to be measured by their ability to foster genuine human service and responsibility.

If there is merit, then, in this analysis of Christian belief from the perspective of the development of human consciousness, I think we are justified in seeing in the Christian mutation of the axial period the emergence of Christian individuation. Just as the axial period is the axis of all individuated humanity, so the resurrection belief can be seen as the axis of Christian individuation. With this it may seem as though nothing more need be said, but several questions still remain. For one thing, human consciousness has continued to develop, and we must ask what possible expansion in self-understanding this development promises for the Christian believer. Further, the development of the non-Christian axis still remains a puzzling one for Christianity, and we will query what relationships are possible between the Christian and non-Christian. And finally, questions of a more metaphysical nature emerge from this kind of analysis—namely, if resurrectional consciousness is initiated by Jesus, what does this imply about him? These we will briefly study in later chapters of this work.

Notes

1. James P. Mackey, *The Problems of Religious Faith* (Chicago, 1972), pp. 190-191, seems to be saying something similar: "Most people . . . have difficulty relating religious faith to history because they can think of faith only as the result of special revelatory experiences of God or of his call; they feel consequently that the concept of special divine revelation is the primary one, or at least they give this impression; and then, as an end result, they find that they have the greatest difficulty in explaining what, in man's historical experience, an instance of self-authenticating divine revelation could have been or could be. But suppose that, instead of talking about history as revelation, we began to talk, at least *began with talk,* about faith as history, or part of history? Suppose that we consistently talk and think of faith as one of the approaches of the human spirit to reality, of reality to the human spirit, and we consequently give primacy to the concept of faith in the analysis of all that can be thought or said in this area?"

2. For helpful critiques of the historico-critical method, see Walter Wink, *The Bible in Human Transformation* (Philadelphia, 1973); James M. Robinson and Helmut Koester, *Trajectories through Early Christianity* (Philadelphia, 1971); and M. D. Hooker, "Christology and Methodology," *New Testament Studies* 17 (1970-71) 480-87.

3. Tracy, *op. cit.,* p. 75. Also cf. pp. 49-52 and 72-79 for an excellent overview of hermeneutical theory.

4. Perhaps Ricoeur means something similar to our "imaginative" hermeneutics in his distinction between a text's "sense" (its written, ideal meaning) and its "reference" (the understanding of our life for which it serves as a catalyst). He speaks of this "reference" as "a sort of being-in-the-world unfolded in front of the text," and further, borrowing from Heidegger: "I want to take this idea of the 'projection of our own-most possibilities' from his analysis and apply it to the theory of the text. Actually, what is to be interpreted in a text is a proposed world, a world that I might inhabit and wherein I might project my own-most possibilities." Cf. Paul Ricoeur, "The Hermeneutical Function of Distanciation," *Philosophy Today* 17 (1973) 129-141, esp. 139 and 140. Ray L. Hart, *Unfinished Man and the Imagination* (New York, 1969), has perhaps most fully articulated the imaginative hermeneutics I have in mind.

5. Voegelin, *op. cit.,* Vol. 1, pp. 428-515.

6. 1 Sam. 9:1—10:16 and 11 is "royalist" and tries to legitimate Israel's conventionalizing; 1 Sam. 8, 10:17-27, and 12 is "anti-royalist" and probably due both to a nostalgia for the pre-conventional, nomadic days and to the later prophetic, post-conventional consciousness.

7. In addition to Cobb, *op. cit.,* pp. 94-106 and Voegelin, other works suggestive of our interpretation are Walther Eichrodt, *Man in the Old Tes-*

tament (London, 1966); G. Ernest Wright, *op. cit.*, and Erich Fromm, *You Shall Be as Gods: A Radical Interpretation of the Old Testament and Its Tradition* (New York, 1966).

8. Cobb, *op. cit.*, p. 99.

9. Eichrodt, *op. cit.*, p. 21.

10. *Ibid.*, p. 23.

11. Voegelin, *op. cit.*, Vol. 1, p. 482.

12. *Ibid.*, p. 485.

13. Cf. esp. Gerhard von Rad, *Old Testament Theology*, 2 vols. (New York, 1962 and 1965). Also helpful is Gerhard Hasel, *Old Testament Theology: Basic Issues in the Current Debate* (Michigan, 1972).

14. Eichrodt, *op. cit.*, p. 27. Cf. Mircea Eliade, *The Myth of the Eternal Return* (New Haven, 1971).

15. Cobb, *op. cit.*, pp. 73-93, for an excellent analysis. Corroborative of Cobb's unreferenced treatment is John H. Randall, Jr., *Plato: Dramatist of the Life of Reason* (New York, 1970), pp. 36-54, 55-79; Jaspers, *The Great Philosophers: The Foundations, op. cit.*, pp. 15-31; Bruno Snell, *The Discovery of Mind* (New York, 1960); and John H. Finley, Jr., *Four Stages of Greek Thought* (Stanford, 1968).

16. Cobb, *op. cit.*, p. 75.

17. Richardson, *op. cit.*, p. 27.

18. Cobb, *op. cit.*, p. 91.

19. Benjamin I. Schwartz, "Transcendence in Ancient China," *Daedalus* 104 (1975) 57-68.

20. Cobb, *op. cit.*, p. 109.

21. I see no reason, from this developmental perspective, to dispute what is a major thesis of contemporary biblical criticism—namely the difference between the pre-Easter Jesus who stands, albeit radically, within the prophetic line as fully God-centered, and the "post-Easter" Jesus "who has become the Christ" and the object of devotion for the early Christian community. Our gradualist approach to development lends further confirmation to the thesis of a pre-Easter Jesus, while the new level of consciousness initiated by the risen one points out why Jesus himself has become the object of devotion. The question of whether the pre-Easter Jesus can be retrieved through historical reconstruction is ultimately a question of the philosophy of history. Gordon D. Kaufman, *Systematic Theology: A Historicist Perspective* (New York, 1968), pp. 185-186, n. 9, has helpfully said: "Many biblical scholars claim it is problematic whether much of significance can be reliably recovered about the historical Jesus. Are we then faced with the alternative either of deserting a responsible historical methodology in order to assert by fiat that certain essential facts about Jesus can really be known . . . or of falling back on the New Testament 'portrait of Christ' as our standard, eliminating the question of whether this portrait has any actual historical referent (the way out suggested by such diverse and weighty thinkers as Barth, Bultmann, and Tillich)? The former way is intellectually irresponsible; the latter is perilously close to Gnosticism. I do not think it necessary to accept either alternative. Both rest on a falsely objectivist conception of historical knowledge, according to which the historian is seeking to lay hold of some objective event-in-itself behind all the documents, an event which is what it is quite apart from all interpretations of it. The first alternative says it is possible to do this, and that therefore we can discover the basic outlines of the person

and career of Jesus; the second declares that, in view of the fact that all our reports were written under the transformative impress of the Easter faith, it is not possible to get such an 'objective' picture of Jesus. Both views however . . . are determined by a view of historical knowledge as essentially concerned with this recovery of the event-in-itself as though the latter were waiting somewhere, like a yet undiscovered planet, to be perceived by the eye of the historian."

22. Cobb, *op. cit.,* p. 111.

23. Cf. esp. Joachim Jeremias, *The Prayers of Jesus* (London, 1967); Tracy, *op. cit.,* pp. 119-145; and Reginald H. Fuller, *The Foundations of New Testament Christology* (New York, 1965), pp. 102-141.

24. Mackey, *op. cit.,* p. 196; he adds, "The man of disillusionment speaks apocalyptic language, the man of confidence speaks prophetic language, but in times of increasing stress the latter imperceptibly shades into the former." I find Fuller's insight only partly correct: "Jesus thought of his own mission not simply as one in the prophetic series, but as the final mission, bringing God's last offer of salvation and judgment" (*op. cit.,* p. 129). Mackey's view more adequately accounts for both elements in Jesus' ministry—namely that of finality and that of incompleteness.

25. Part of the difficulty here is the meaning of "factual." The resurrection, as I believe, transcends the factual *as we know it,* and is thus not open to historical verification. What are so open, with more or less probability, are the resurrection *appearances.* For details, see C. F. Evans, *Resurrection and the New Testament* (London, 1970); Gerald O'Collins, *The Resurrection of Jesus Christ* (Pennsylvania, 1973); and the very perceptive articles of Edouard Pousset, "La resurrection," *Nouvelle revue théologique* 91 (1969) 1009-1044 and "Croire en la Resurrection," *ibid.,* 96 (1974) 147-166, 366-388.

26. To my mind it is insufficient to claim that the "objective pole" was Jesus' death, and that the resurrection was simply the result of the "creative, cognitive dissonance" of the disciples, as Hugh Jackson holds in his "The Resurrection Belief of the Earliest Church: A Response to the Failure of Prophecy?" *Journal of Religion* 55 (1975) 415-425. O'Collins, *op. cit.,* pp. 31-32, gives three objections to this: (1) the resurrection belief is new and not simply explicable in terms of previous Jewish or Hellenistic belief; (2) the evidence points to disappointed and crushed disciples, not creative and enthusiastic ones; (3) the appearance to Paul, three years after the supposed event, puts an untolerable strain on a simply subjectivist theory.

27. To my mind, the most satisfying is that of Pousset, *art. cit.* From my own Christian perspective, the key reason for the disagreement over the nature of the resurrection resides in the fact that it transcends the empirical world as we know it. As Thomas Aquinas long ago observed, the Christian resurrection does not refer to the resuscitation of a corpse. Were this the case, and apart from the question of whether this resuscitated person were dead in the strictly theological sense, we would again be dealing with an empirical reality observable to the senses. Rather, as Aquinas observed, "Christus resurgens non rediit ad vitam communiter omnibus notam, sed ad vitam quandam immortalem et Deo conformem" (*Summa Theologiae,* 3, 55, 2). Cf. Gerald O'Collins, "Thomas Aquinas and Christ's Resurrection," *Theological Studies,* 31 (1970) 512-522. There exists, then, no empirical fact

against which we can test our notion of the resurrection. The same difficulty, of course, occurs when we are dealing with any notion referring to a trans-empirical reality—for instance, "God," "soul/psyche," "world," etc. The issue, then, is not simply an empirical one, but turns on more fundamental philosophical and anthropological considerations. One's ultimate vision of man is the key issue, and all such "ultimate issues" cannot be verified by empirical and thus direct tests, but only indirectly—by asking, for example, whether one's vision enables one to deal with every dimension of human experience. Cf. the helpful comments of Kaufman, *An Essay on Theological Method, op. cit.,* pp. 71-72, where he treats of the issue of theological construction and truth.

28. In some oblique ways, even the New Testament sees in the resurrection the beginnings of a new kind of consciousness. For example, the risen Jesus could only be recognized after the disciples had attained a new level of awareness (Lk. 24:16, etc.). Paul himself saw in the resurrection a new basis for understanding human destiny (1 Cor. 15:14-15, 17). The Gospels summarize this new vision by their use of the "third day" motif, for the "third day" was the traditional day of victory and deliverance (cf. Gen. 22:4; 42:18; Ex. 19:11, 16; Hos. 6:1, etc.). In other words, even for the New Testament the resurrection was bound up with a new development in self-awareness or consciousness. In fact, one could make a case that the various interpretations of the resurrection throughout the Church's history vary directly with the manner in which the resurrection is seen as altering man's own self-consciousness. John Navone, *A Theology of Failure* (New York, 1974), pp. 31-32, put it well: "The various orthodox explanations of the Christ-event derive from particular dimensions of the risen Christ's impact upon human experience. For example, the new vision of reality, created by the experience of the risen Christ, is the basis for an attempt to explain the Christ-event in terms of enlightenment. Clement of Alexandria taught that the incarnate Logos illuminates the believer with his own incomparable light. Athanasius and Cyril of Alexandria wrote eloquently of Christ as the light of the world and as the giver of the Spirit of truth, transforming mankind through enlightenment. . . . There was no single formulation of the doctrine of the Christ-event in the patristic period. The exemplarist tradition tends to describe the impact of the risen Christ primarily in terms of moral regeneration, a redirection of the human spirit. The Western liturgical tradition tends to view it in terms of what Christ's self-sacrifice has achieved for others. The Eastern liturgies express the impact of the event as a *rescue* and a *healing*. . . . Every model that serves to explain how man may enjoy life more fully illuminates the experienced meaning of the risen Christ among his people."

29. Richardson, *op. cit.,* p. 26. Richardson maintains that all the axial leaders discovered this insight. As I have tried to argue throughout, I think it is necessary to distinguish between the various axial leaders and the kinds of awareness of a transcendent reality that emerged in consciousness.

30. I would like to indicate my reliance upon Henri I. Marrou, *The Resurrection and Saint Augustine's Theology of Human Values* (Villanova, 1966). While Marrou translates the resurrection belief into the human values it implies, I translate it into the view of selfhood it implies. It is a further question as to what this resurrection belief implied for man's physical or bodily makeup. In normative Christianity the radically spiritual view of selfhood

was not seen as negating man's body, but as freeing it from any tendency toward disorder. Christian belief in the resurrection of the body presupposes a consciousness which is aware that man's physical self is not destroyed but transformed by the spiritual self. Because Greek thought identified the spiritual self with reason, a resurrection belief did not emerge in Greece. Rather, the *soul's* immortality (i.e., the immortality of reason) became the dominant belief in Greek philosophy.

31. Cf. O'Collins, *The Resurrection of Jesus Christ, op. cit.,* pp. 101-106.

32. *Ibid.,* p. 104.

33. Cobb, *op. cit.,* p. 117. Cobb, in fact, sees this as the distinctive mark of Christian existence. It led, in his view, to a new focus on the divine as "Spirit" in Christianity. Cobb likes to maintain that the prophetic discovery of God-as-Father led to the emergence of "personal existence," while the Christian discovery of God-as-Spirit led to the emergence of "spiritual existence" or radically self-transcendent existence. My focus on the resurrection has led me to see greater continuity between Judaism and Christianity than Cobb sees.

34. *Ibid.,* p. 122.

35. Eliade, *op. cit.,* pp. 160-161.

36. Neumann, *op. cit.,* p. 221.

37. *Ibid.,* p. 249.

38. *Ibid.,* p. 221.

39. Cf., for what follows, Ernst Käsemann, "For and Against a Theology of Resurrection," in *Jesus Means Freedom* (Philadelphia, 1970), pp. 59-84.

40. It would appear that the only resurrection belief Voegelin knows is the distorted one of the Corinthians. See his *Order and History,* Vol. 4, *op. cit.,* "The Pauline Vision of the Resurrected," pp. 239-271.

41. Cf. Mackey, *op. cit.,* pp. 173-181, for a good analysis.

42. Mircea Eliade, *The Myth of the Eternal Return, op. cit.,* is the classic on this question.

43. In this light, W. Thüsing's remark bears further investigation: "The belief in Christ is not a lessening, but a qualitatively new radicalizing of the Old Testament Yahweh-monotheism and its correct, intensive, and emphatic confession, 'Hear, O Israel, your God is one.' New Testament Christianity is rather . . . a belief which brings out the deepest significance of the Old Testament and makes it fulfilled in a new way." Cf. his and Karl Rahner's *Christologie—systematisch and exegetisch* (Freiburg, 1972), p. 228 (my translation).

44. Cf. the classic study of Ernst Käsemann, "Ministry and Community in the New Testament," *Essays on New Testament Themes* (London, 1968), pp. 63-134.

45. Cobb, *op. cit.,* p. 118.

46. Evans, *op. cit.,* pp. 150-151.

47. Cf. Günther Bornkamm, *Paul* (New York, 1971), pp. 31-42.

IV
The Problem of Christ's Divinity in the Light of Christian Consciousness

Introduction: The Problem of the "Shift"

What can helpfully be explored at this point is what Christians were led to affirm about Jesus and why they did so. Here the hypothesis I wish to pursue is that the early Christian affirmations about Jesus were a function of their new level of consciousness and unintelligible except in its light. Interpretations vary on the validity and significance of the affirmations that later Christians came to make about Jesus. But no serious scholar questions the fact that the New Testament witnesses to a shift of concern, from Jesus' radical stress on Yahweh and his Kingdom, to Jesus himself. Gordon Kaufman puts it succinctly:

> The most that could be said historically is that the Christian Church is a community which explicitly and openly believes that in some decisive fashion God manifested himself in these particular events [of Jesus], that is, it believes its *historical* ground to be its true *ontological* ground.[1]

This new concern for Jesus himself eventually led the New Testament authors to assert some rather strong claims for Jesus: "There is no salvation in anyone else, for there is no other name in the whole world given to men by which we are to be saved" (Acts 4:12). "No one has ever seen God. It is God the only Son, ever at the Father's side, who has revealed him" (Jn. 1:18). "Everything has been given over to me by my Father" (Mt. 11:27). As Raymond Brown[2] helpfully illustrates, this new focus on Jesus eventually took its decisive step in naming Jesus

85

"God": "In the beginning was the Word; the Word was in God's presence, and the Word was God" (Jn. 1:1). "Thomas said in response, 'My Lord and my God'" (Jn. 20.28). Speaking of the Son, the Epistle to the Hebrews affirms, quoting Psalm 45, "You have loved justice and hated iniquity: therefore, O God, your God has anointed you with the oil of gladness" (Heb. 1:9).[3]

A number of interesting insights emerge from Brown's analysis. First, he is only able to isolate, with historical probability, the three above texts which clearly name Jesus "God." Why are the texts so few, and why so late, since all of these texts are found in the latest layers of the New Testament? Brown's view: "The most plausible explanation is that in the earliest stage of Christianity the Old Testament heritage dominated the use of the title 'God'; hence 'God' was a title too narrow to be applied to Jesus."[4] Brown is probably most helpful, then, in clarifying why Jesus was not termed "God." His analysis forces us to recognize that the eventual naming of Jesus as "God" was a late development whose ambience was originally liturgical. Thus we must speculate that this decisive step in the history of religions witnesses to a development on the part of the early Christian disciples themselves, and the goal we have set for ourselves in this chapter is to see to what extent our analysis throughout this book might clarify why this decisive step was taken.

Problems in Evaluation

One manner of evaluating this dramatic "shift" in the New Testament is made possible by our historically and transculturally conscious epoch. Since Max Müller's monumental series, *Sacred Books of the East,* in the nineteenth century, scholars have created a new specialization known as *comparative* religions.[5] This comparative approach to religion has enabled many scholars to note a striking similarity between the New Testament's gradual process of ascribing deity to Jesus and similar "deification" processes in other religions, Oriental as well as Hellenistic. This approach has won a somewhat favorable hearing from some New Testament scholars, and most notably has been employed by the famous exegete Rudolf Bultmann. Although each scholar employs this comparative method in his own unique way and so with his own unique nuances, the basic notion is that religious history indicates that founders of religions tend to be "deified" by their followers the more removed those followers are from their original founders. Herbert Stroup, for example, in his comparative study of the world's living religions stemming from known founders, has noted this deifying process at work in all of them:

> The founder is assumed to be divine through the process of deification. It is true that the founders of religions have refrained from claiming their own divinity. At times they have specifically asserted that they are thoroughly human. They have even denied the claim of their disciples that they are exceptional, saying that only God is good. But their followers do not accept their views. The followers traditionally respond to the heroic lives and noble teachings of their founders by worshiping them as gods. Even those founders who denied the existence of the gods or God end up becoming gods.[6]

One of the more common manners of utilizing this insight in New Testament studies is to note the parallels between Christian affirmations of Jesus and affirmations, for example, as found in the Greek mystery religions, and then to argue for intercultural borrowing. Hans Jonas' view that Christianity stems from Gnosticism is one such example. Bultmann's attempt to note certain parallels between Pauline theology and the Greek mystery religions is another. We will later note our disagreement with Jonas, arguing that Christianity is neither in its origins nor in principle Gnostic. And further, while there is a great deal of evidence to support intercultural borrowing, especially as Christianity spread into the Hellenistic world, the difficulty is that the parallels are never exact and seem rather to point in the direction of a transvaluation in meaning of the Hellenistic materials.[7]

However, intercultural borrowing does not really take us

to the heart of the matter. What Stroup and numerous others[8] have perceived is that the tendency to "deify" a religion's founder is a deep-seated one, built into the fabric of the religious mind itself. Christmas Humphreys, in his own attempt to account for the differences between Theravada Buddhism, which originally avoided deifying the Buddha, and the Mahayana school, which exhibits many of the features of our deification tendency, is probably not wide of the mark in ascribing the latter to a deep-seated psychological need: "Certainly the fundamental distinction seems to be that between the emotions and the mind, of Bhakti Yoga as distinct from Jnana or Karma Yoga."[9] What Humphreys is pointing to is one of the fundamental characteristics of religion—its ability to satisfy the whole person, body, emotions, and mind. Deifying the founder is one of the ways in which we fulfill this fundamental need. It brings the goal of our aspirations close to us, places God within history, and gives reality to our dreams, as Feuerbach would have said.

Of course, if this is how one understands early Christianity's deification of Jesus, then the problem is raised beyond the level of historical studies, with its attempt to detect intercultural borrowing. The issue at once becomes more philosophical and has to do with the question of whether such a process is legitimate at all. In keeping with my own perspective, which is not that of metaphysics, but of attempting to clarify what metaphysics seeks to establish—meaning rather than truth, to employ the distinction of linguistic analysis—what might we say about this deification process?

As described by Humphreys, the deification tendency can be understood, in our terms, as an archaic tendency, a lapse into a pre-axial phase of consciousness. As we recall, primitive man dwelled in a numinous world, a world of sacrality and divine immediacy. This is not difficult to understand, for every child dwells in the same kind of world. Because the child's experience is undifferentiated, and thus lacking in the clear ability to distinguish subject from object, his world is also numinous and full of mystery. Only as the child's sense of individuation develops, and thus his ability to distance himself from nature and to understand it critically and reasonably—

only in this way does nature lose its sacrality and numinous nature. Now what makes Humphreys' case is that this experience of the numinous and of divine immediacy is something that the religious man seeks to recapture. We need little proof of this, what with all the renewed interest in the occult and astrology occurring in our times. The point, then, is that, irrespective of whatever intercultural borrowing we may be able to discern in the New Testament, the gradual veneration and eventual deification of Jesus can be seen as one of many examples of a lapse into a pre-axial, mythical mode of consciousness.

But while the above view perhaps confirms the views of many that the Christian claims for Christ cannot be maintained by anyone who has overcome the mythical way of thinking—or at least "relativized" it through rational thought—a further possibility exists. Prior to exploring this possibility in my own terms, I would like to refer the reader again to the thought of James Mackey, which I would regard as structurally equivalent to my own. Mackey helpfully distinguishes between the language of faith and the language of revelation. The former results from *man's* side, from his expansion of consciousness, and speaks from man's side: "I believe . . . I acknowledge that . . . I confess." As Mackey clarifies it, "Such language is as characteristic of that area of human psychic reaction known as religious faith, as is language containing the word 'ought' of man's moral reaction to reality."[10] In my terms, this is the kind of language which results from a religious expansion of consciousness. As it gives expression to a human experience, it is fully defensible in terms of that experience, even to axial and rational people. Revelation-language speaks *from God's side,* however: "Thou shalt not," etc. This is the kind of language widely found in the New Testament: "*God* raised Jesus from the dead," "God sent forth his only Son," etc. What I find important in Mackey is his assessment of this latter kind of language:

It is absolutely essential, as witness its place in the great religious traditions. The very conviction of religious faith calls for it, with an inner need that can be satisfied by nothing else. The very intensity of my faith conviction

. . . cannot find adequate expression except in terms of
. . . speech which is as from God's side. . . . Especially
in the case of those person-centered events, such as the so-
called Christ-event, which inspire religious faith in men
and give that faith a very distinctive orientation within the
world, men find it absolutely necessary to say that God
acted in such an event and such people.[11]

For Mackey, then, revelation-language need not *necessarily* be
a lapse back into a pre-axial mentality. It can also be a descrip-
tive, metaphorical manner of giving expression to a new level
of consciousness, occasioned by a certain religious experience
of reality. "All revelation talk is a metaphorical or mythical
description of the literal truth of faith, as necessary and justified as myth itself is necessary and justified, as in fact the
only way we have of talking about God at all."[12]

Mackey's insights, as well as my own perspective, have led
me to distinguish two distinct kinds of mythical consciousness.
It is true that the ascription of divinity to Jesus may be a lapse
back into a more archaic mode of thinking, much as any adult
regresses back to childhood when he allows himself to get lost
in an unbeneficial fantasy world. This kind of mythical thinking is incapable of making adequate distinctions, of bringing
fantasy under control by rational thought. But just as psychologists envisage the possibility of a "regression in the service of
the ego," so we can envisage, not precisely a regression into an
archaic mode of thinking, but a recapturing of myth, but this
time purified and relativized by an axial consciousness. We
have already seen an example of this in Cobb's analysis of the
new outbreak of the "Spirit" following the resurrection appearances. As the Corinthian experience illustrated, this did indeed
signify, at times, a lapse into a more archaic mode of awareness. However, Paul relativized this mythical enthusiasm by
placing it in the context of and at the service of love and
human responsibility (1 Cor. 12). Indeed, there was a new experience of the mythical sense of divine immediacy and the
numinous following the resurrection appearances, although it
was a purified one, manifesting not a loss of responsible personhood, but its complexification and fulfillment. As we hope-

fully recall, human development is a *complexifying* process, and previous modes of awareness are not annulled but continue, and are thus capable of resurfacing in more responsible ways. And so the possibility remains that the resurfacing of revelation-language in the New Testament stems from this complexified mythical awareness and is one of the ways in which the early Christians gave expression to their new and deepened experience of divine immediacy made possible by Jesus. The later history of Christology indeed can be interpreted as the Church's struggle with a more archaic mode of thinking, but I also think it is defensible to maintain that the healthier sort of myth always won the day, at least in principle.[13] This possibility of a responsible use of myth may well be one of the factors underlying the strong language used of Jesus. Spelling out what that might further mean is the goal we have set ourselves in the rest of this chapter.

A further attempt at an explanation of the New Testament deification tendency has been classically referred to as the "Hellenization of dogma," at least since the time of Harnack. A well known theory, it attempts to account for the deification language in the New Testament by viewing it as the result of intercultural borrowing from the Hellenistic culture. While a very good case can be made for this sort of borrowing, as all are aware, the theory breaks down when it is advanced as a *total* explanation of the origins of the New Testament "high Christology," as it is sometimes called. The evidence, on the contrary, would argue for a "Christianization of Hellenism," rather than the so called "Hellenization of Christianity." Perhaps a few examples may help in making this clear. What makes the case for the Hellenization theory is the early Christian use of such terms as "Lord," "Christos," "Son of God," etc., which can be paralleled in Hellenistic sources, but what should not be overlooked is that the New Testament subjects Greek thought to a thorough transvaluation in meaning: Hellenistic polytheism (Gal. 4:8) is replaced by Hebraic monotheism (1 Cor. 8:6); the Gnostic heavenly forces are under God's dominion (Col. 1:16, 20); Hellenistic dualism and emanationism is rejected; Hellenistic self-salvation and fate is replaced by a sense of hope and God's graciousness; even John's

Gospel, the most thoroughly Hellenistic and "Gnostic," subjects both to a radical critique. What Fuller says of John 1:14, could be applied to the Hellenistic theory itself: it "is only possible within Christianity, and as a result of the history of Jesus of Nazareth."[14] In the face of these difficulties, my own suggestion—shared by many in one way or another—is that we are dealing here with a development in the disciples themselves. I use the word "development" decidedly, because, of course, many would argue that it was not a "development" at all, but at best a "change" and at worst a "regression." To explain this I would have to refer the reader back to my (admittedly partial) explanation of the resurrection appearances as initiating a new quality of consciousness. That new quality of consciousness can be variously expressed. Gordon Kaufman's own superb formulation I find most appealing: "Thus was born a new awareness of the authentic meaning of human existence and a new hope for the future movement of human history."[15] In terms of my own analysis, the resurrection belief witnessed to a consciousness which lived in terms of a transcendent source of identity, relativizing the oppressive powers of this world. This gave the early disciples a new awareness of the meaning of Jesus' career and death, as well as a new and decisive understanding of human life itself. As Nietzsche correctly saw, it involved a transvaluation in human meaning:

> Modern men, with their obtuseness as regards all Christian nomenclature, have no longer the sense for the terribly superlative conception which was implied to an antique taste by the paradox of the formula, "God on the cross." Hitherto there had never and nowhere been such boldness in inversion, nor anything at once so dreadful, questioning, and questionable as this formula: it promised a transvaluation of all ancient values.[16]

If the resurrection belief witnesses to a consciousness that believes that God has acted in some decisive fashion in Jesus and opened up decisively new possibilities for human existence, then we are enabled to view the resurrection as an event resulting in a developed and expanded consciousness in the disciples themselves. Most basically, and in its earliest form, I would see this new resurrectional differentiation of consciousness as lying behind the great claims made for Jesus, as well as behind the new outbreak of the "spirit" and the restoration of the formerly mythical divine immediacy.

What we are saying, then, is that this expanded consciousness of the disciples witnessed to a development in themselves, a kind of deepened differentiation of consciousness. I wish to stress that this was a "development," bringing about a greater ability on the disciples' part to penetrate the significance of Jesus and his ministry. In this light it is somewhat beside the point as to whether Jesus himself made any great claims for himself, and equally beside the point is the attempt to revert to a pre-Easter understanding of Jesus.[17] The difficulty with each is that it allows no space for development, growth, and increased understanding. Just as the adult more deeply understands the child because of the growth in his own experience, so too can we not say that the disciples' deepened growth in experience led to an equally deepened understanding? Development means more, not less, understanding.[18]

Further, as we formerly noticed that the resurrectional consciousness led to a new outbreak of the "Spirit" and thus a restored and transformed experience of divine immediacy, so, too, perhaps we can understand that this new experience of the Spirit was behind the disciples' ability to see God's decisive action in Jesus. As John explains it, the Spirit will enable the disciples to understand the truth about Jesus (Jn. 16:13). Or, in Paul's terms: "No one can say 'Jesus is Lord,' except in the Holy Spirit" (1 Cor. 12:3). Divine immediacy had been *restored* in the Christian consciousness, but it had also been *transformed,* in accordance with the axial level of consciousness which Jesus initiated. For that divine immediacy had been seen first and foremost in the *cross of Jesus,* and thus in a life of fully individuated self-responsibility:

Man could now see for the first time that ultimate reality is not to be understood simply in terms of the all-too-human conceptions of worldly power, the ability to achieve what one wants regardless of obstructions or handicaps thrown in the way. The cross could never be made to symbolize that. On the contrary, in the cross were found meekness and submission, non-resistance to evil, self-sacrifice; and the resurrection meant that just this cross was the very revelation of God's innermost nature and his mode of action with the free spirits he had created in history.[19]

Hopefully this explanation of the matter enables us to understand Mackey's view about the appearance of revelation-mythical-language in the "high Christology" of the New Testament. I would be inclined to think that the naming of Jesus as "God" is primarily to be understood in this transformed sense of mythical thought. Incidentally, this enables us to further understand Brown's[20] view that this language probably developed primarily in a liturgical context, for a worshiping context is precisely the most favorable one for a restored sense of divine immediacy. But by allowing room for development, as this theory does, we can perhaps more fully understand some later developments in Christology also.

In addition to the expansion of consciousness made possible by the resurrection belief, there is an ordinary expansion of consciousness which results simply from the further intensification of individuation itself. As the "ego" is able to distance itself from reality and critically reflect upon it, there emerges that abstractive ability which, we have said, characterizes the Greek axial breakthrough. While this was most developed in Greek thought, it is a normal outgrowth of human development itself. In terms of Kohlberg's views, which we have utilized throughout, it is the kind of thinking characteristic of the post-conventional person in which the individual asks *ultimate* questions about the nature of reality: various cultures and groups say such and such about reality, but what is really and ultimately the case? Culturally, as we have seen, this was a late development in man's history, for it presupposes a highly developed abstractive ability, one through which the individual can distance himself both from the immediate and the cultural and raise ultimate questions. Granted this, it should come as no surprise that early Christianity began to reflect upon Jesus in this more sophisticated manner, partly as a result of its entry into the Hellenistic world, but partly also as the result of its own human maturation itself.[21] The early Church would first have to gain distance from Jesus' own immediacy, as well as distance from what various cultural groups had to say about him, before it could engage in this kind of reflection.

It should come as no surprise, then, that the later Church, particularly in its patristic era, engaged in this more reflective and metaphysical speculation about Christ. And I suspect that one's *final* evaluation of the patristic and scholastic Christological achievements greatly depends upon whether one accepts a developmental view of man in which ultimate questioning is accorded its legitimate place. I would personally maintain that the early Church was not mistaken in its attempt to philosophically probe the significance of Christ and to translate its mythical sense of God's immediacy in Christ into doctrines of Christ's "natures" and "person."[22]

A Clarification from Gordon D. Kaufman[23]

This view, then, that the doctrine of Christ's divinity is a function of the Christian differentiation of consciousness, and that it expresses, in extrapolated form, the Christian awareness of ultimacy in Jesus, only tries to clarify how that doctrine arose. My purpose, though, has been to show that a developmental view of human consciousness can give an adequate account of that matter, and that the Christian need not accept indefensible views about the origins of this doctrine. One such view, that Gordon Kaufman has done much to clarify, is the idea that the disciples visibly "saw" God in Jesus: "The earliest disciples did not visibly see God in Jesus. . . . The doctrines of the incarnation and the deity of Christ are *theories* . . . intended to interpret the central *fact* of which the disciples (and the subsequent Church) were convinced, namely that here *God—* the ultimate limit of our existence and the ultimate reality with which we have to do—is encountered, not merely man."[24] From the point of view of our own analysis, this makes good sense.

For, first, if God is really a transcendent God, this being could not then be one of the many objects of this world observable to the senses. This would actually deny divine transcendence, and in any case we have maintained that the disciples, rather than "seeing" God in Jesus, *theorized* to the conclusion of God's presence from their own expansion of consciousness. Further, this view makes sense of the Christian claim that Jesus "reveals" who God is. Rather than *a priori* and *a-historically* deciding what a divine being is, and then seeing whether Jesus "fits" this description, this view maintains that the early disciples only came to an awareness of divinity historically, as a result of their experience of Christ.

Notes

1. Kaufman, *Systematic Theology: A Historicist Perspective, op. cit.,* p. 179.
2. Cf. Raymond E. Brown, "Does the New Testament Call Jesus God?" in his *Jesus: God and Man* (Milwaukee, 1967), pp. 1-38. While Brown concentrates on whether the New Testament authors ever attribute "deity" to Jesus with the same meaning as when attributed to Yahweh, Karl Rahner had concentrated on why these authors generally did not refer to Jesus as "God." Cf. his *"Theos* in the New Testament," *Theological Investigations,* Vol. 1 (Baltimore, 1961), pp. 79-148. Both Rahner and Brown independently agree.
3. Brown's translation, *op. cit.,* p. 24.
4. *Ibid.,* p. 33.
5. Cf. A. C. Bouquet, *Comparative Religion* (Baltimore, 1971), pp. 20-36, for a brief overview of the history.
6. Herbert Stroup, *Founders of Living Religions* (Philadelphia, 1974), p. 30.
7. See our next section on the Hellenization of doctrine. Cf. also Rudolf Bultmann, *The History of the Synoptic Tradition* (New York, 1963), for the Hellenization thesis, and Fuller, *op. cit.,* for a persuasive dissent.
8. Cf., among others, Gustav Mensching, *Das Wunder im Glauben und Aberglauben der Völker* (Leiden, 1957), where throughout he traces religion's tendency to lapse into superstition *(Aberglauben).* Hippolyte Delehaye, *The Legends of the Saints: An Introduction to Hagiography* (Notre Dame, 1961), has masterfully traced an analogous tendency in Christianity.
9. Christmas Humphreys, *Buddhism* (Baltimore, 1962), p. 51.
10. Cf. Mackey, *op. cit.,* p. 191; cf. pp. 190-206 for this section of my chapter.
11. *Ibid.,* pp. 191-192.
12. James P. Mackey, "The Theology of Faith: A Bibliographical Survey (And More)," *Horizons* 2 (1975) 235.

13. The question of how to adequately explain this new sense of divine immediacy is a further issue, but it should not be *a priori* maintained that it is indefensible. Hopefully, the rest of this chapter will lend some clarity to the matter. For the moment it is helpful to quote Mackey, "The Theology of Faith," *art. cit.*, 235: "Next, if Jesus has inspired faith in me, must not my acknowledgment comprehend Jesus in its range if it is to be true? In less historical terms, is not my acknowledgment of God simultaneously acknowledgment of his world; never a purely theoretical affair, always a practical cherishing, enjoyment, commitment in hope? What else then, in actual historical terms, can my acknowledgment now be except simultaneous acknowledgment of Jesus, following him in practice, discipleship? And as I would say in any case of God's word that it is his gift, communication, revelation, how else can I speak truly of Jesus (since, by inspiring this radical faith he has put me in the right relationship to God) except as God's word, God's revelation? These are metaphors, of course, but when I speak of things below or above my human state I can only speak metaphorically, mythically, in a word, anthropomorphically. I have no other way of telling the truth. Faith is literal, revelation talk metaphorical."

14. Fuller, *op. cit.*, p. 224.

15. Kaufman, *Systematic Theology: A Historicist Perspective, op. cit.*, p. 431.

16. *Beyond Good and Evil* (Chicago, 1959), as quoted by Kaufman, *op. cit.*, p. 432.

17. Much as Oscar Cullmann thinks. See Fuller, *op. cit.*, p. 257, n. 1.

18. Cf. Avery Dulles, *Apologetics and the Biblical Christ* (Westminster, 1964), p. 68: "Whence did the apostles derive their conviction that Jesus was Lord over all creation, sharing with his Father in the government of the universe? If we wish to accept the apostles' own account of their faith, we shall have to say that it was not simply a matter of assenting to what Jesus had expressly said of himself in his earthly existence. Still less was it a logical inference." The difficulty with the first is that it allows no room for development; with the second, that it misconceives the nature of development, viewing it as primarily logical-deductive, while I view it as a process of complexification, in which deepened experience brings to the surface, through a process more complex than logic, new data incapable of being known or deduced without that deepened experience.

19. Kaufman, *Systematic Theology: A Historicist Perspective, op. cit.*, p. 432.

20. Brown, *op. cit.*, pp. 34-38, esp. 37: "The liturgical ambiance of the New Testament usage of 'God' for Jesus also answers the objection that this title is too much of an essential definition which objectifies Jesus and is untrue to the soteriological interest of the New Testament. As far as we can see, no one of the instances we have discussed attempts to define Jesus essentially."

21. Fuller, *op. cit.*, pp. 248-249, hits on this: "It may, of course, be argued that this ontic language [i.e., the New Testament high Christology] is merely the translation into Greek terms (and mythological terms at that) of what the earlier functional Christologies were affirming. This is true, but it is not the whole truth. For it is not just a quirk of the Greek mind, but a universal human apperception, that action implies prior being—even if, as is also true, being is only apprehended in action. Such ontic reflection about Yahweh is

found even in the Old Testament, e.g., 'I Am' (Exodus and Deutero-Isaiah)."
The ability to ask ontic questions presupposes the abstractive ability which
characterizes the post-conventional individual.

22. Some careful studies: Alois Grillmeier, *Christ in Christian Tradition,*
Vol. 1 (Atlanta, 1975); John Meyendorff, *Christ in Eastern Christian
Thought* (Washington, D.C., 1969); and Per Erik Persson, *Sacra Doctrina:
Reason and Revelation in Aquinas* (Philadelphia, 1970), esp. pp. 191-224, for
Aquinas' Christology.

23. Kaufman, *Systematic Theology: A Historicist Perspective, op. cit.,*
pp. 176-189.

24. *Ibid.,* p. 183.

V
Soteriology in the Light of Christian Consciousness

Our last chapter engaged in a kind of "backward" movement: from the Christian expansion of consciousness *back to Christ* himself. Now we would like to propose a "forward" movement: from that same consciousness *to us*. Here we will be considering the theme known traditionally as "soteriology," the question of what Christ has done for mankind, or, put in Luther's famous terms, the *Christus pro nobis*. Again we will consider this from our own perspective of consciousness and seek to clarify the meaning of soteriology from that vantage point. Our hypothesis is, by now, a familiar one: just as the doctrine of Christ's divinity emerged in function of the Christian consciousness, so, too, the belief in Christ's redemptive work was in function of that same consciousness, and unintelligible without it. What we mean can be initially clarified by some helpful comments from John Dunne. Referring to the "illumination of mind" which is equivalent to our "expansion of consciousness" resulting from each new phase of human development, he speculates:

> Illumination of the mind occurs not so much through the acquisition of new information as through the discovery of a new standpoint from which the available information can be regarded. Each new life experience, as a man goes from age to age or from phase to phase, is the occasion for a new understanding of things.[1]

Such is how we have sought to understand each of the breakthroughs in human consciousness. The Hebraic discovery of God was not just some new item of information but a discovery so fundamental that it reoriented the entire quality of

Hebraic life. Individuality and human autonomy became genuine possibilities, history in the sense of man's having an open future really emerged in consciousness, and, most importantly, the sense of being absolutely loved, as expressed in Jeremiah's new covenant of the heart, was born. The work of Jesus, as we have sought to show, did not annul any of these gains, but deepened them by revealing the full extent of human individuation and responsibility made possible by life under God. But an "illumination" of the mind or an "expansion of consciousness" only partly explains what was going forward in these breakthroughs. Dunne again can be of help here: "The new understanding he attains is in itself an illumination of the mind, but it becomes also an inspiration of the will if he finds in it a new basis for action, if the new standpoint becomes a new plane of existence."[2] In our terms, each new increment in consciousness opens up new possibilities for human existence and thus becomes a new basis of action. Soteriology, we could say, is simply the attempt to conceptually explain the new basis for action opened up by the resurrectional expansion of consciousness.

The Christian notion of soteriology, then, was originally an insight which emerged from the Christian expansion of consciousness. Like all previous breakthroughs in human consciousness it led to more, not less, insight into the structure of reality. This is why I have consistently referred to a resurrectional consciousness as an expanded consciousness, for it enabled the early Christians to imagine the possibility of a fully individuated existence under God. By bringing into awareness the final implications of a transcendent source of personal identity, it relativized every limit and thus revealed that full individuation is indeed a possibility within the world. This expanded insight into the structure of reality probably accounts for the exuberant confidence of Paul, and there exists no finer example of our axial individuated self-responsibility than this text:

Who will separate us from the love of Christ? Trial, or distress, or persecution, or hunger, or nakedness, or danger, or the sword? . . . For I am certain that neither death nor life, neither angels nor principalities, neither the present nor the future, nor powers, neither height nor depth nor any other creature, will be able to separate us from the love of God that comes to us in Christ Jesus, our Lord (Rom. 8:35-39).

In this Pauline text we can see clearly how the resurrectional consciousness opened up not only an illuminated mind, but also a new basis for action. This insight into a new basis for human action lies behind the Christian notion of redemption.

Just as the Christian notion of redemption was in function of the Christian consciousness, so *all* notions of "redemption" are in function of human consciousness. Actually, "redemption" itself is not an a-historically fixed notion, but rather one that has developed in meaning as man's consciousness itself has developed. "Redemption," understood in the sense we are using here as the possibility of full human individuation in God, could not even be imagined by a pre-axial mentality. It is because Hebraic and Christian men became aware of themselves as *individuals* in function of their reflection upon God and upon Christ that the possibility of human individuation emerged in man's consciousness. In the pre-axial mind, the goal of life would be conceived in terms of a harmony with nature or an adherence to conventional rules and customs, but not in terms of individuation. It is this latter which is distinctive about the Christian notion of redemption. This comes out in Christian reflection upon both sin and freedom.

On John Cobb's[3] analysis, the New Testament evidences a very sophisticated, axial, understanding of both sin and freedom. As we have seen, the prophets, through their axial understanding of God, developed a very sophisticated understanding of human responsibility. The God who asked for obedience and moral conversion implied a responsible man capable of giving them. But in general there were felt to be limits to this responsibility, and man was felt to be responsible "primarily for voluntary actions."[4] Christian reflection on the nature of man, however, appears to be much more sophisticated and witnesses to an attempt to take into account man's "involuntary actions," the inner resistances which led him in the direction of sin. Paul's formulations are classic:

> I cannot even understand my own actions. I do not do what I want to do but what I hate. . . . I act against my own will. . . . This indicates that it is not I who do it but sin which resides in me. . . . The desire to do right is there but not the power. What happens is that I do not the good I will to do, but the evil I do not intend (Rom. 7:15-19).

This Christian stress on the "involuntary" in man could have led to a negation of the axial sense of responsibility which we have said characterizes Christianity, but it did not. It rather led to a deepened and radicalized understanding of responsibility:

> The Christian experienced himself as radically responsible for himself beyond the point of his actual apparent ability to choose. Here is the seat of the rationally perplexing but existentially powerful understanding of original sin. . . . Somehow the Christian knew himself as responsible for choosing to be the kind of self he was, even when he found that his desire to change himself into another kind of self was ineffectual. Hence, he must shift his efforts from a direct struggle to alter himself to the attempt to become open to the work of the divine Spirit that could do within him something which he could not do in and for himself.[5]

In other words, Christianity was able to move in the direction of a radicalized notion of sin, precisely because it radicalized the sense of human responsibility. The new sense of responsibility made possible by his resurrectional consciousness fostered in him the ability to take responsibility for and to transcend even the involuntary dimensions of human existence. This is why Cobb refers to Christian existence as one of "self-transcendence.[6] When redemption is spoken of in the New Testament, it is primarily this new consciousness of being in possession of a way to deal with sin that is in mind (Rom. 3:24; 1 Cor. 1:30; Eph. 1:7; Col. 1:14; Heb. 9:15). Not even death is an obstacle: "Death is swallowed up in victory" (1 Cor. 15:54). Of course this new consciousness could be expressed positively, for a freedom from sin is at the same time greater freedom (Gal. 5), peace, and reconciliation between God and man (Rom. 5:10; 11:15; 2 Cor. 5:18; Col. 1:20). But my key point is only to bring home that the Christian notion of redemption is an axial one. Rather than negating human individuation and responsibility, it demands it and makes it possible.

At the same time we find in the New Testament the resurfacing of pre-axial notions of redemption.[7] These have always proved a perplexity to scholars, precisely because their pre-axial nature has not been noticed. For example, Christ's salvific work is alternately described as a "ransom" (Mk. 10:45) or as a kind of legalistic saving (Heb. 5:9), or it is described liturgically as a *sacrifice* (Eph. 5:2; Heb. 9:25), an *expiation* (Rom. 3:25), or as a shedding of the blood for many (Rom. 5:9; Heb. 9:12). When taken in isolation, these texts tend to reduce redemption to a kind of juridical and legal transaction on Christ's part and thus collapse the axial sense of individuality and responsibility radicalized by Jesus. From the viewpoint of our own analysis, these descriptions of redemption are the "cultural mortgages" of a conventional mentality in which life is understood primarily in legalistic and ritualistic terms. What Christ initiated was not seen as the fostering and intensification of human individuation, with all that implies, but rather man understood the redemptive act in terms of a pre-individuated phase of existence, much as the conventional Hebrews understood the goal of their existence as adherence to the legal prescriptions of the covenant. Historically, Anselm's satisfaction theory, heavily influenced by Roman law, can be understood as the classical attempt to systematically explain redemption in these legal, conventionalized categories. Whatever the many good things that can be said about it, it does not bring out the axial sense of individuation that primarily characterizes Christianity.

The key difficulty, I think, is in missing the point that while pre-axial notions of redemption resurface in the New Testament and later, all of these notions have been transformed by the prophetic and Christian entry into axial consciousness. Redemption is neither some legal act performed by God nor some legal adherence to conventional modes of behavior on man's part, but the possibility of fully individuated and responsible existence. Paul's struggle with the Corinthians and Judaizers can be taken as establishing this fact *in principle*.[8] But while the quality of consciousness underlying the Christian view of redemption is a fully axial one—at least in principle—the evidence would seem to indicate that it has been understood in primarily pre-axial, archaic ways until recent times. In part this can be explained as the result of the mass conversions of primarily pre-axial peoples since the time of Constantine. In part, also, it is due to the lack of an historical self-consciousness through which the cultural mortgages of the past have been finally overcome and man is confronted with the need to take full responsibility for himself. It is this latter element which, more than any other, lies behind the attempted revisions of the Christian notion of redemption since the nineteenth century. Each[9] is an attempt to recapture the properly human sense of individuation and responsibility initiated by Jesus. Of course, in a self-conscious age, the great danger is that religion will be reduced to a purely human phenomenon. However, I will try to show later that self-consciousness can lead to a maturation of the religious consciousness, too, in which religion is seen as the development of fully individuated responsibility under God.[10] Further, I will also try to show that the chief merit of our current transcultural age will be, I think, to summon forth even more deeply this sense of individuation made possible by Christian belief.

Notes

1. Dunne, *op. cit.,* p. 116.
2. *Ibid.*
3. Cobb, *op. cit.,* pp. 119-123.
4. *Ibid.,* p. 120. Cf. John L. McKenzie, "Sin," *Dictionary of the Bible* (Milwaukee, 1965), p. 818: "There is never any question in the Old Testament whether sin is a deliberate and willful act for which man must bear full responsibility. There is no suspicion of any compulsion or neurosis, nor any failure of society which excuses the individual. Sin is indeed a breakdown

of society, and the prophets often speak of this; but society breaks down because of the failure of its members."

5. *Ibid.*, p. 121. This was already implied in the prophetic breakthrough (*ibid.*, pp. 119-120).

6. *Ibid.*, p. 124; cf. p. 123: "A new level of transcendence appeared. The self became responsible for the choice of the center from which it organized itself and not only for what it chose from a given center"; also cf. p. 124: "The essential demand of God has to do precisely with those dimensions of selfhood which the personal 'I' cannot control. To accept those demands and to accept responsibility to live in terms of them is to accept radical responsibility for oneself, and that is, at the same time, to transcend one's self. That means that the new spiritual 'I' is responsible both for what it is and for what it is not, both for what lies in its power and for what lies beyond its power. For the spiritual 'I' need not remain itself but can, instead, always transcend itself. Thus, spiritual existence is radically self-transcending existence."

7. Cf. Gustaf Aulén, *Christus Victor: An Historical Study of the Three Main Types of the Idea of the Atonement* (London, 1970); Kaufman, "The Christ-Event. The Atonement," in *Systematic Theology: A Historicist Perspective, op. cit.,* 389-410; and Joseph F. Mitros, "Patristic Views of Christ's Salvific Work," *Thought* 42 (1967) 415-447.

8. Aulén, *op. cit.,* misses this point in his positive assessment of the "ransom" theory of redemption.

9. Cf. Kaufman, *Systematic Theology: A Historicist Perspective, op. cit.,* pp. 402-403, n. 10, for the famous nineteenth-century liberal view; for the attempt to further this development more critically, see Francis Schüssler Fiorenza, "Critical Social Theory and Christology: Toward an Understanding of Atonement and Redemption as Emancipatory Solidarity," *Proceedings of the Catholic Theological Society of America* 30 (1975) 63-110.

10. Curiously enough we find a partial recapturing of the axial view of redemption in Abelard who sees how Christ's redemptive work fosters human individuation: "The unique act of grace . . . frees us from slavery to sin" by evoking a "deeper affection . . . so that we do all things *out of love* rather than fear—love to him who has shown us such grace that no greater can be found" (italics mine). Cf. his *Exposition of the Epistle to the Romans,* Commentary on Rom. 3:19-26, *Library of Christian Classics,* Vol. 10 (Philadelphia, 1956), pp. 283-284.

PART III
DEVELOPMENTS
IN
CHRISTIAN CONSCIOUSNESS

VI
Christianity, Historical Consciousness, and the Problem of the Autonomous "Ego"

Distanced from us as the axial period is, we are in a position to assess its crucial importance for the quality of our lives today. The word "axial" is not ill chosen if indeed that age discovered the possibility of authentic human individuation. Eric Weil has said: "The idea of an axis suggests a revolving movement."[1] Exactly, for to the extent that we ourselves want to be individuated beings, with the freedom and autonomy that entails, we will have to "return" to the axial period and relive its breakthroughs. But our distance from the "axis" permits us a view forbidden to the people who actually lived through it. Just as the adult can see the strengths *and the limits* of adolescence, as the axial man could see the strengths *and the limits* of pre-axial people, so perhaps we too are in a position to assess *the limits* of the axis. After all, our analysis points to a man's increasing complexification and differentiation. Each new phase expands man's awareness and possibilities. The evidence indicates that this complexifying process has continued, and from its vantage point a further assessment of the axis seems called for.

Voegelin has spoken of mortgages which are imposed on movements by the historical circumstances of their origin. Robert Bellah[2] has devoted some attention to this question, and his conclusions might offer us some insights into the limits of the axial period. His short but lucid critique of the axis, which for him is the era of the "historic," not "mythical," religions, begins with what he sees as the fundamental discovery of that age—namely the "transcendental." Previously we spoke of Benjamin Schwartz' view that what characterized the axial leaders is the "strain toward transcendence." Schwartz concentrated on the etymological meaning of "transcendence": a standing back and looking beyond, a critical questioning, and a creation of a new vision beyond. Like Schwartz, we too concentrated on this "transcending capacity" and maintained that its development brought into being the highly individuated and differentiated self capable of distancing itself and calling into question both its immediate and cultural environments. Bellah mentions this aspect also:

> From the point of view of these religions a man is no longer defined chiefly in terms of what tribe or class he comes from or what particular god he serves but rather as a being capable of salvation. That is to say that it is for the first time possible to conceive of man as such.[3]

But Bellah's concentration brings into focus the axial tendency toward what he terms "dualism," and the subsequent history of religions certainly proves him correct. We recall that the axial leaders discovered a realm of meaning transcending the immediate and the cultural. The prophets' discovery of a transcendent Yahweh, Jesus' immediacy to Yahweh through his radical stress on the kingdom, Greek thought's eventual crystallization in the Platonic "Ideas," the Tao of the Orient, the critique of rationality in Buddhism—all such transcendent visions and perspectives fostered "dualism"—that is, the tendency to derogate the historical for the sake of the transcendent. Thus, Bellah says, "The discovery of an entirely different realm of religious reality seems to imply a derogation of the value of the given empirical cosmos; at any rate . . . world rejection . . . is, in this stage for the first time, a general characteristic of the religious system.[4]

From our perspective we could say that in a pre-conventional and conventional framework, religion tends to be this-worldly or, in Bellah's words, "focused on this life." This should be easy enough to see, for in these frameworks one takes his clues for interpreting his identity either from nature or from society. In the axial religions, however, religious concern "now tends to focus on life in the other realm, which may be either infinitely superior or, in certain situations with the emergence of various conceptions of hell, infinitely worse."[5] According to Bellah this leads to a stratified hierarchy which represents this new "sacred" and "transcendent" realm over against the "laity." Because of this dualism, separating "this" world from the one really important "transcendent" one, the crucial issue which comes to the fore is *salvation*. Further, this new transcendent realm fosters the feeling that man is separated from his true home, and one of the primary tasks of religion is to understand this sense of inner separation and alienation. Buddhism thus speaks of this world as an "illusion"; the prophets see man's wickedness not just in particular evil deeds but in the totality of his life, and Christianity finally crystallizes in Augustine's notion of "original sin." Bellah's final assessment seems important at this point:

> Perhaps partly because of the profound risks involved, the ideal of the religious life . . . tends to be one of separation from the world. . . . The early Christian solution, which, unlike the Buddhist, did allow the full possibility of salvation to the layman, nevertheless in its notion of a special state of religious perfection idealized religious withdrawal from the world. In fact the standard for lay piety tended to be closeness of approximation to the life of the religious.[6]

How are we to evaluate Bellah's critique of the axial period? From our perspective it is a rather formidable one which seems to be confirmed by later religious history. If it stands correct, without further qualification, it would seem to deny what was a central thesis of our last chapter—namely that the axial breakthroughs, particularly the Christian differentiation, fostered the emergence of full, this-worldly self-responsibility. Dualism, in Bellah's sense, on the contrary, would foster escapism from this-worldly responsibility.

I think we are provided a first clue for our evaluation of Bellah's critique by John Cobb's analysis of Gnosticism.[7] Cobb's description of Gnosticism seems very similar to Bellah's notion of "dualism": "Gnosticism is here understood as that movement of the later Hellenistic world which sought salvation from the whole cosmos regarded as, in principle, an alien and evil power."[8] Since, in Gnosticism, the "cosmos" includes man's body and soul, Cobb distinguishes it from prophetic and Christian existence. The latter he regards, as we do too, as basically man-affirming.

When one reads the Gnostic literature, he immediately recognizes a great amount of mythical thinking.[9] Yet Cobb understands it as a basically axial phenomenon, and thus a movement reflecting the shift to the dominance of rational thinking. However, what distinguishes Gnosticism from both prophetic and Christian existence is the fact that it represents people who were "thrust out of" pre-axial existence, not so much by a gradual transition to the more differentiated plane of axial existence, but rather more violently by the imperialism of the Hellenistic empires. What this imperial expansion fostered was not so much a complete differentiation into axial existence, but a partial differentiation in which mythical thinking was not rejected but overlaid with a rationalistic interpretation. Voegelin's independently researched *The Ecumenic Age*, by the way, tends to confirm Cobb's analysis.

Gnostic teaching simply reflects such a partial or "mixed" differentiation. As we recall, what partially characterized the conventional phase of human existence—the era of the great civilizations—was a tension between the mythical and the rational, together with what each represents. The mythical, with its sense of immediacy and its numinous experience of the world was threatened by rationality. The latter seemed to alienate man from his need for participating in nature and experiencing the sacred.[10] On Cobb's analysis, this sense of alienation was intensified when pre-axial peoples were thrust into axial existence by foreign domination. Such, for example, was the case with the Hellenization of Egypt and Syria. The Gnostic myths simply reflect this intensified alienation by their hostility toward a world which they greatly resent. Thereby, this "sense of alienation . . . created a consciousness of self or spirit as something wholly other to all the rest of the psychic life."[11] The Gnostic "I" sensed itself as different from the world and as yearning for something that the world cannot offer.

Thus it is no accident that Gnosticism occurred only among those for whom Hellenization was occurring. The "Hellenic culture," in distinction from the "Greek culture," represents the mixture and fusion of axial and pre-axial elements. Thus we find Gnostic elements among both the Greeks and the Hebrews, for both underwent this Hellenization process. The Greek mystery religions and Gnostic elements in the New Testament may be seen as examples of this. Cobb sees in stoicism, with its ruthless suppression of nature, a harbinger of Gnosticism, for it basically reflects the latter's sense of alienation from the world. The step from Stoic hostility to the world to Gnostic condemnation of the world was not a great one, but when the step was taken, the peculiar Gnostic "I" emerged. Jewish apocalypticism, when it met with a pre-axial, Hellenized person, could also lead to Gnosticism, and thus we find the latter among the Hellenized Hebrews.

Perhaps Cobb's analysis of Gnosticism provides us with a partial explanation for the dualism stemming from the axial period. Gnosticism, with its world condemnation, perhaps represents an extreme form of the dualism which Bellah is pointing to as latent within the axial period. Perhaps the same factor which generated Gnosticism lies behind all dualism in general —namely the fact that pre-axial peoples were thrust into axial existence without being prepared for it. To my mind this seems highly characteristic of later Christian history, particularly from the time of Constantine's conversion. The "mass conversions" resulting from that event likely included large numbers of pre-axial peoples. The later development of Buddhism and Taoism in a Tantric direction and the shift from Platonism to Neo- and Middle Platonism perhaps point in the same direction. In any case, the evidence does not indicate that the Hebraic and Christian differentiations were per se dualistic in Bellah's sense of world derogation. Paul's struggle with the Corinthians and the early Church's condemnation of Gnosticism would seem to argue against this. Perhaps this is why Bellah speaks only of a "tendency" toward dualism. Christianity presupposes the axial awareness of personhood and responsibility, but when this is lacking, as it clearly was among pre-axial Christians, then Christianity runs the danger of being pushed in a Gnostic, world-denying direction.

Nonetheless, possibly a deeper reason exists for the tendency toward world-denying dualism, and an exploration of this may help us understand why the dualistic tendency became so prevalent, despite the Church's condemnation of Gnosticism. What I am referring to is the lack of what we have come to call today an "historical consciousness." The latter, as scholars generally recognize today, only began to emerge between the thirteenth and seventeenth centuries. Herbert Richardson describes it in this way:

> At the second axial transition, a transition occurring between the thirteenth and seventeenth centuries A.D., a further complexification of human consciousness takes place. Man becomes *self-conscious*. He begins to reflect upon his own consciousness and to become aware of *himself* as its free and active cause.[12]

Once we understand why this further development in human consciousness took so long to emerge, we will be in a better position to evaluate the dualism of the axis.

An historical consciousness calls for an "axial mind" and something more. It requires an "axial mind" because it *requires a highly developed reflective ability,* an ability to distance oneself from the order of historical events and, once distanced, to reflect upon what is implied by those events. However, it requires something more, too. After all, Aristotle wrote some profound analyses of history, thus exemplifying the highly sophisticated reflective capacity we have in mind. Yet we do not consider Aristotle historically conscious. Aristotle was truly aware of historical change, but not in the same way that we are today. He was aware that people are born, that they grow old, and die. He knew of the existence of previous generations, and thus of the reality of historical change, even cultural change. But what he did not know and could not know was the radically historically conditioned nature of human existence.

The historical sciences as we know them could only emerge much later, after the lapse of much more history, after the recording of that history in records, and after the availability of those records to later generations.

The story of the emergence of historical consciousness is a fascinating one in its own right. For our purposes, though, it is only important to underline a few of its details. According to Norman Hampson, the events occurring during the Renaissance and Enlightenment gradually opened up a new dimension of time.[13] What the thinkers of this time were beginning to consciously grasp was that man makes his own history. A new dimension of "time" opened up, for time was no longer thought to be simply the earthly reflection of an eternally decreed blueprint, but the genuine result of human striving itself. A first example of time's new dimension was the view of time that the physical sciences were developing. Montesquieu, as a result of his geological studies, questioned the accuracy of the Bible's six thousand year chronology of the world. When he was later proven correct, even the Bible was seen as the result of time-conditioned, human self-making. Further, Maupertuis, through his biological studies, developed a theory of genetic transmission, hinting at the existence of dominant and recessive characteristics in the human organism. This clearly pointed to the historically-conditioned makeup of even man himself, albeit from a biological perspective.

The new dimension of time opened up by the physical sciences was paralleled in the historical sciences. Indeed, it is because of the new awareness of history coming to the fore at this time that we date the emergence of the historical sciences as such from this period. An important impetus to this awareness was the quest for discovery and travel, which enlarged European horizons beyond Europe and revealed the historically conditioned nature of human culture. As a result of such travels, Voltaire could say, in reference to China: "Authentic histories trace this nation back . . . to a date earlier than that which we normally attribute to the flood."[14] Again, the scriptural chronology was seen to be only one, culturally conditioned view of human history. Further, a new use of historical texts came into prominence during the Renaissance and early

Enlightenment periods. As we know, few ages witnessed a return to the writings of classical Greece and Rome as enthusiastic as that of the Renaissance, but this was not a lapse into archaism or a simple nostalgia for the past. These texts were being used critically, evidencing a sense for historicity. The past was no longer simply an authoritative source to which to appeal, but a source to be critically evaluated by historical methods. This procedure, of course, increasingly called into question the a-historical use of the biblical texts by ecclesiastical authorities. Peter Gay has summarized well the new historical sense that was emerging:

> The historians of the Enlightenment . . . at least . . .
> freed history from the parochialism of Christian scholars
> and from theological presuppositions, secularized the idea
> of causation and opened vast new territories for historical
> inquiry. They went beyond tedious chronology, endless
> research into sacred documents, and single-minded hagi-
> ography, and imposed rational, critical methods of study
> on social, political, and intellectual developments.[15]

If we want a brief indication of what this new awareness of time means, we need only compare Bossuet's seventeenth-century brand of history as the unfolding of the eternally decreed with Vico's view of the same as "the developing self-knowledge of societies, which became increasingly aware of their ability to control their material environment and to influence the complex of assumptions and attitudes which is misleadingly described as 'human nature.'"[16]

The historical consciousness of which Richardson spoke above is the direct heir of the Renaissance and Enlightenment. The story of the historical sciences is too well known to retell in depth. From our perspective, what is important is to underline the complexification in human consciousness that it brings about. An historically conscious individual presupposes a new and deepened awareness of oneself: man becomes aware of himself as a self-creative being. For the historical and physical sciences point to the fact that man has altered and can alter both nature—through scientific and technological manipulation

—and himself—through a similar self-imposed transformation. Nature and man are both open to radical alteration. Man could not have had this deepened awareness of himself when history was thought to be rather more static and inflexible. But there can be little doubt that this new self-awareness on man's part has come into its own in our day. Just as I am doing, Jaspers devotes the entire middle section of his *The Origin and Goal of History* to this new awareness, and with his usual acuity, he describes its implications well:

> In Greek thought the answer to a question always arises from deliberation and plausibility, in modern thought from experiment and progressive observation. In the thought of the ancients an investigation meant simply meditating on the problem; only in modern thought does it come to imply action.[17]

What this means is that man is now increasingly aware of himself not simply as an object of reflection, but as a subject, a self-creative being capable of altering both nature and himself. There can be little doubt that axial man knew himself as an object of reflection. Axial man's break from myth presupposed man's ability to differentiate himself from external reality and thus to become aware of himself as an "I." However, he knew himself rather more as an object than as a self-creative subject. Axial man did develop rather extensive analyses of himself. The role of the new covenant "of the heart" in Jeremiah and Ezekiel, the New Testament's emphasis on interior motive (the heart), Paul's intricate anthropology (the body, the spirit, the flesh)—all of this reflects the sense of individuation which is the lasting legacy of the axial period. Indeed, these analyses of man became rather developed and intricate in Hinduism and Buddhism. Perhaps this was because the Orientals entered into the axial period, not through an increasingly rationalized understanding of God, but through a direct confrontation with the self as individuated, yes, but also isolated and alienated.[18]

Christianity, too, eventually developed similar analyses in its monastic tradition, in which the quest for personal salvation was primary. It is out of this that the intricate analyses of the stages of the spiritual life developed in early Christian mysticism.[19] I would personally maintain that the Christian mystical literature reflects, in a heightened manner, the stages of the development of human individuation which are the subject of this chapter. Since the quest for personal salvation was the mystics' avowed and explicit goal, their writings clearly reflect the axial sense of individuation, and indeed presuppose a high degree of it. But just as we are maintaining that the Renaissance witnesses a shift in human development, in which man becomes aware of himself more as a self-creative subject than simply as an object, so, too, the mystical literature from this date exemplifies the same shift. Luther knows himself rather more as a subject capable of altering the course of events than as a simple object. So, too, the writings of a Teresa of Avila and Ignatius Loyola seem to illustrate the Renaissance emphasis on subjectivity.[20]

In any case, the new sense of subjectivity can be seen in less opaque and more transparent ways in contemporary developments. Technology, with its ability to manipulate nature and create the synthetic or artificial, presupposes man's awareness of himself as a self-creative subject. Contemporary philosophy's turn to the subject, in which man is recognized quite consciously as a symbol-creating being and the determiner of what counts as a value for himself, illustrates the same point. Contemporary psychology and psychoanalysis are explicitly based on the notion that man can render his own subjectivity transparent to his consciousness and alter it in accordance with his own vision of what man should be. The contemporary discovery of the category of the "social," in which society is seen as the product of human self-making and thus open to analysis and possible alteration, is the foundation of the contemporary social sciences.[21]

This deepened awareness of the self as a self-creative subject means that the conscious "I" of the axial period has become self-conscious. Today's individuated man not only knows he is an "I," but he also knows that the "I" that he is and will become is largely the result of his own self-making. This, of course, necessarily heightens the sense of responsibility which emerged in the axial period: responsibility becomes a quite conscious *self*-responsibility. Similarly the sense of freedom and autonomy is heightened: it becomes more burdensome, but it also opens up greater possibilities of human development.

When man becomes aware of himself as a self-creative subject, this awareness, if thought through, overcomes the world-denying dualism which Bellah finds in the axial period. It is no longer a question of two worlds—a transcendent one and a this-worldly, earthly one—but of one world, the world to which man chooses to commit himself. This collapse of dualism is the feature which Bellah himself singles out in his own analysis of contemporary religion:

> At the highest intellectual level I would trace the fundamental break with traditional historic symbolization to the work of Kant. By revealing the problematic nature of the traditional metaphysical basis of all the religions, and by indicating that it is not so much a question of two worlds as it is of as many worlds as there are modes of apprehending them, he placed the whole religious problem in a new light.[22]

What Bellah's analysis enables us to grasp is that, even were the Gnostic tendency toward dualism lacking, the axial religions would still tend toward a world-denying dualism because of the lack of an historical consciousness. Kant's discovery, which represents the discovery of historical consciousness, is that man's worlds of meaning are his own self-creation. Prior to this awareness one would tend to think in terms of the two-world schematism: this earthly one of man and the transcendent one proclaimed by the axial leaders.

In terms of the development of human and Christian consciousness, it would seem that our new historical consciousness can precipitate two quite distinct developments. On the one hand it can lead in the direction of a humanism or man-centeredness. The discovery that man's worlds of meaning are his own self-creation heightens the awareness of the centrality of the self. Raimundo Panikkar has expressed this rather well:

> Discovering the laws of the cosmos he also discovers his own *nomos* and becomes more and more aware that his mind, his *nous,* is the criterion of intelligibility and perhaps even of reality. After wondering at nature he wonders at his mind and is awe-struck to see how the physical universe seems to follow the laws which his mind discovers and is able to formulate.[23]

Historically this has led to an emphasis upon, and even a glorification of, man's reason. Descartes' *res cogitans* became the new axis of human existence. The Enlightenment's glorification of reason was critiqued, it is true, by Freud and Marx and their heirs. They attempted to show that the emphasis upon reason was naive, omitting the irrational factors in human existence. But even for Freud and Marx human reason remained the one real hope for man. They did not replace the centrality of reason, but freed it from the Enlightenment's naiveté.

As I hope to show later, today's emphasis upon the self has led to an acknowledgment of the self-aware individual as the one ideal and hope for man. Curiously this leads in the direction of alienation, for as man becomes more aware of his own individuality and its self-creative powers, he becomes more lonely, forced to depend solely upon himself. Historically the Greek axial breakthrough could have led in the same direction. The Greek conception of *moira* partly inhibited the full glorification of reason, and I personally think that the Christianization of Greek thought ultimately blocked reason's enthronement. This is of some importance. Since the Hebraic and Christian entry into axial consciousness was a function of belief in God, the idolization of the human self was not really a possibility. Both Hebrews and Christians knew they were not simply self-dependent or self-reliant, but recognized that individuality was a possibility because of the divine initiative. This emphasis upon the divine initiative not only inhibited a creed of self-reliance, it also inhibited the alienation and loneliness to which that creed gives rise. Hebrews and Christians surely knew what loneliness was, but this loneliness was never radicalized, simply because they entered into axial existence in function of their belief in the divine presence. Gnostic consciousness was a radically alienated and lonely one, but this was never the normative experience in Christianity. However, to the extent that today's heightened self-consciousness tends in the direction of humanism and a loss of the awareness of the divine presence, there will be nothing left to inhibit the only other alternative left to man: self-reliance, and, with it, the isolated and lonely autonomous individual.

I personally think that, as the Oriental axis becomes more and more Westernized, the problem of the alienated individual will become theirs also. As I sought to show earlier, loneliness is one of the fruits of entering into axial existence. As the individual differentiates himself and becomes aware of himself as an "I," this necessarily brings with it the awareness of being different and separated from the undifferentiated wholeness of mythical experience. The Orient experienced this loneliness in a heightened way, but I do not think it was a radicalized experience equivalent to today's experience. What so far has inhibited this more radicalized alienation in the Orient is the effective presence of what Voegelin would call the "mythical mortgages" of the Oriental axis. The mythical fosters a numinous experience of reality, which I think has so far been sufficient to avoid the radicalized autonomy of Western man. Westernization, however, will increasingly call the mythical experience of the numinous into question.

The real difficulty for the humanistic trend, then, is whether it represents a real gain beyond the axial period, one which will ultimately not destroy but complexify and deepen the axial discovery of self-responsible personhood. Panikkar has perhaps pinpointed humanism's difficulty: "Individualization can only become an ideal if man finds in his individuality the fullness of all that he can be—otherwise it would be an intolerable impoverishment."[24] We will return to this question in our final chapter.

As we have sought to show throughout, what ultimately accounts for every breakthrough in human consciousness is an intensification of elements previously present. Thus, the intensification of man's rational capacities underlies the axial breakthrough. Today's historical consciousness is a further intensification of that same rationality. However, if my analysis of the humanistic trend bears merit, we may be witnessing, not an intensification but an exaggeration and idolization of but one element in the full human psyche. In any case, it would seem that an authentically Christian response to historical consciousness would be born from an awareness of this possible danger. The task for the Christian consciousness today must be a complexifying one—that is, neither annulling the gains of the axial period nor of our self-conscious age, but integrating them into a more complexified consciousness. This means, as Pannikkar put it, that the Christian must "regain on a second level or a higher turn of the spiral"[25] the gains of the axial period. What would this mean?

Basically, this more complexified consciousness would seek to avoid the error underlying the cult of individualization. The latter replaces the dualistic, two-world schematism, which was a tendency of the axial period, with a simple monism: the cult of autonomous reason. In this light, Bellah's insight into the contemporary problematic seems more realistic and more in accord with the total history of the development of human consciousness: "It is not so much a question of two worlds as it is of as many worlds as there are modes of apprehending them."[26] And more poignantly:

> In the world view that has emerged from the tremendous intellectual advances of the last two centuries there is simply no room for a hierarchic dualistic religious symbol system. . . . This is not to be interpreted as a return to primitive monism: it is not that a single world has replaced a double one but that an infinitely multiplex one has replaced the simple duplex structure. It is not that life has become again a "one possibility thing" but that it has become an infinite possibility thing.[27]

The difficulty is that the idolization of autonomous reason, precisely by being monistic, is incapable of accounting for the full range of possibilities open to human consciousness. Our analysis of human consciousness would seem to argue in a fashion similar to Bellah. Precisely for its own self-realization human consciousness would seem to confirm the Judaeo-Christian axis. This, of course, does not destroy the place of reason, but it does relativize it and argue for its inadequacy as a total explanation of human consciousness.

In writing this chapter I have found that I have arrived at conclusions remarkably similar to those of Erich Neumann in his stimulating study of the history of human consciousness. He, too, has noted our contemporary problem of the emergence of autonomous reason:

> Just as the differentiation of conscious functions in the individual harbors in itself the danger of overdifferentiation and one-sidedness, so the development of Western consciousness as a whole has not escaped this danger. The question now arises of how far conscious differentiation can proceed and where it begins to turn into its opposite; that is, at what point . . . there arises the danger of a mutation which . . . will lead to his downfall.[28]

But most illuminating for our purposes is his diagnosis of the effects of this overdifferentiation. In Neumann's view, two quite different processes can be set in motion by this phenomenon. On the one hand, he variously speaks of "possession," "inflation," or the "regression to the unconscious." That is, when the rational function of consciousness becomes so predominant that the self loses contact with other aspects of the personality, there occurs "an activation of the deeper-lying layers [of the self] which, now grown destructive, devastate the autocratic world of the ego with transpersonal invasions, collective epidemics, and mass psychoses."[29] Overstressing the rational dimensions of the self leads the non-rational component to overcompensate. On the other hand, he speaks of a "sclerosis of consciousness," "deflation," and "the isolation of individualism." As he explains it, "In a sclerotic consciousness . . . the autonomy of the conscious system has been carried so far that the living link with the unconscious becomes dangerously atrophied."[30] In his view the form of degeneration usually occurring in the West is this very sclerosis "where the ego identifies with consciousness as a form of spirit. In most cases this means identifying spirit with intellect, and consciousness with thinking."[31]

Quite clearly what Neumann hopes for is the restoration of a balanced form of human consciousness. In his view that will have to take the form of a rapprochement with the unconscious, since in his Jungian view the latter is the final source of the non-rational components of human selfhood: "No outward tinkerings with the world and no social ameliorations can give the quietus to the daemon, to the gods and devils of the human soul, or prevent them from tearing down again and again what consciousness has built."[32]

I am not, of course, a Jungian, and I do not view the ultimate task to be one of only a rapprochement with the unconscious.[33] However, what I do see of utmost value in Neumann's own analysis is the need for as holistic a view of human consciousness as possible. Basically our times are forcing us to ask what it is that will foster the full and total development of the human self. In a study like this, I cannot buttress my views with metaphysical and theological arguments, but my analysis clearly predisposes me toward the Judaeo-Christian form of consciousness as an holistic one, offering man the potential development of the full range of his human aspirations. Because the Judaeo-Christian defines himself in terms of a transcendent source of personal identity, he is potentially able to relativize all things finite. However, the other side of "relativizing" is "totalizing." The refusal to define oneself in terms of partial aspects of reality allows the full range of human selfhood to emerge. Adrian van Kaam seems to have these thoughts in mind when he refers to man's awareness of God as a "totalizing tendency": "It is an aspiration for all that is, for participation in a beyond that generates and encompasses us." And what happens when this aspiration is refused?

[It] returns as a totalizing tendency that has lost its true object. We feel impelled to totalize frantically all kinds of little beyonds that we have made absolute, such as status, money, honor, success, and popularity. We do not know how to overcome these fixations on earthly concerns that wear us out, for we have lost our openness to the original source of all totalizing tendencies: the refused tending toward the absolute and the subsequent aspiration for the Eternal.[34]

I would query, however, whether Christianity has been very successful in presenting and defending the potential for human totalization implied in Judaeo-Christian consciousness. There would seem to be counterparts to Neumann's "regression to the unconscious" and "sclerosis of consciousness" within Christianity itself. The "regressive tendency" manifests itself whenever Christians refuse to strive for the integration of the claims of reason with the rest of their psychic lives. Although, as we have seen, this regressive or archaic tendency can be traced as far back as the Corinthian enthusiasts of Paul's time, it has become especially accentuated in our modern, overrationalistic period. It is no accident that "fundamentalism" and many other anti-rational movements have arisen in Christianity at this time. Equally prevalent is the "deflationary" trend, a sort of Christian sclerosis of consciousness which manifests the modern overdifferentiated ego by identifying consciousness with intellect and thinking. It is instructive for Christians to read these words of a Jungian psychoanalyst:

A good example of this [i.e., the sclerosis of consciousness] is the concept of God which now derives wholly from the sphere of consciousness—or purports to derive from it, as the ego is deluded enough to pretend. There is no longer anything transpersonal, but only personal; there are no more archetypes, but only concepts; no more symbols, only signs.[35]

Notes

1. Weil, *art. cit.,* 21.
2. Robert N. Bellah, "Religious Evolution," in *Beyond Belief* (New York, 1970), pp. 20-50.

3. *Ibid.*, p. 33.

4. *Ibid.*, p. 32.

5. *Ibid.*

6. *Ibid.*, p. 34.

7. Cobb, *op. cit.*, pp. 151-156.

8. *Ibid.*, p. 151.

9. See Hans Jonas, *The Gnostic Religion* (Boston, 1972).

10. Cobb locates the mythical in man's unconscious, following Neumann and Jung. Thus, reason tended to alienate man from his own unconscious. I have sought to avoid this Jungian approach to man's psychic life and thus I am interpreting Cobb in my Piaget-and-Kohlberg-influenced interpretation. Cf. Neumann, *op. cit.*, for the key influence behind Cobb, so far as I can tell.

11. Cobb, *op. cit.*, p. 153.

12. Richardson, *op. cit.*, p. 39.

13. Norman Hampson, *The Enlightenment* (Baltimore, 1968), pp. 218-250.

14. As cited by Hampson, *ibid.*, p. 26.

15. Peter Gay, *The Enlightenment: An Interpretation* (New York, 1966), p. 37. But note his critique on p. 38: "The philosophes' perception of a distinction between mythmaking and scientific mentalities was the perception of a fact, but since they came to it first of all through their position as critics and belligerents, they almost inevitably converted the historical fact into a moral judgment, praising, indeed identifying themselves with, one mentality and denigrating the other."

16. Hampson, *op. cit.*, p. 235.

17. Jaspers, *op. cit.*, p. 87.

18. Cf. Mircea Eliade, *Yoga: Immortality and Freedom* (Princeton, 1969), for the Hindu and Buddhist development.

19. John Meyendorff, *St. Gregory Palamas and Orthodox Spirituality* (New York, 1974), has excellently traced the progressive development of Christian anthropology in the Eastern spiritual authors.

20. What is indicative of this shift in Teresa of Avila and Ignatius Loyola is their analysis of spiritual development *subjectively,* not simply objectivistically. This can be seen by a careful analysis of Teresa's use of the first person singular pronoun in her *Autobiography.* Ignatius illustrates this in his analysis of discernment in his *Spiritual Exercises.* For both, the spiritual life is seen not only objectively as something happening *to* the person, but rather from the point of view of the subject, as something which one quite consciously takes into her or his own control. Cf., among others, Louis Cognet, *Post-Reformation Spirituality* (New York, 1959), and Karl Rahner's exegesis of Loyola in "Being Open to God as Ever Greater," in *Theological Investigations,* Vol. 7 (New York, 1971), pp. 25-46.

21. Cf. H. Stuart Hughes, *Consciousness and Society: The Reorientation of European Social Thought 1890-1930* (New York, 1958).

22. Bellah, *op. cit.*, p. 40.

23. Raimundo Panikkar, "Ecology from an Eastern Philosophical Perspective," *Monchanin* 8 (1975) 25.

24. *Ibid.*, 25.

25. *Ibid.*, 26, and further: "Without lamenting this process (which was probably inevitable) [i.e., the supremacy of *res cogitans*], we may now per-

haps be in a position to complete the spiral and, without lapsing into a kind of naive primitivism, rejoin those loose bits and pieces of reality which today begin to come into focus."

26. Bellah, *op. cit.*, p. 40.

27. *Ibid.*

28. Neumann, *op. cit.*, pp. 383-384, Cf. "The Schism of the Systems: Culture in Crisis," pp. 381-394, for most of this section.

29. *Ibid.*, p. 389.

30. *Ibid.*, p. 384.

31. *Ibid.*, p. 386. The effects this has on human development are worth noting: "If carried to extremes, the differentiating and emotion-repressing trend of Western development has a sterilizing effect and hampers the widening of consciousness. This is confirmed by the fact that creative people always have something childlike and not fully differentiated about them; they are plasmatic centers of creativity, and it is quite beside the point to call such features 'infantile' and try to reduce them to the level of the family romance" (p. 387); and a further effect: "It leads to an overexpansion of the ego, which thereupon tries to demolish the transpersonal by calling it mere illusion and reducing it to personalistic ego data" (pp. 388-389).

32. *Ibid.*, p. 393.

33. In my final chapter I try to express my reasons for this in more detail.

34. Cf. Adrian van Kaam, "Psychodynamics of Spiritual Presence," in *In Search of Spiritual Identity* (New Jersey, 1975), pp. 111-112 (for this citation), and pp. 108-137 (for the entire chapter).

35. Neumann, *op. cit.*, p. 389.

VII
On the Need for a
Transcultural Consciousness

The Present Shape of Religious Pluralism

One of the many merits of Eric Voegelin's *The Ecumenic Age* was to point out that the axial leaders—whether Buddha, Plato, Zoroaster, or Paul—were able to develop a universal view of man precisely because of their historical need to transcend cultural particularity, or, as we would say today, cultural pluralism. The pragmatic empires of the first millennium, with their confluence of many different cultures, needed a spiritual vision to give them unity. As long as man's worth was identified with and tied to the particular culture that nurtured him, this more universal vision of man was blocked. What distinguished the great religions and made them our axis even today was their discovery that the individual is more than a simple miniature or echo of a particular culture. This affirmation of human individuality implied the affirmation of the individual's intrinsic worth as well as the affirmation that his worth transcends cultural boundaries. This is why Eric Weil has said, "It remains true that the great discovery of the first millennium was (for us) the principle of universality, the affirmation that every individual may accede to truth and/or happiness."[1]

As we have seen, the Judaeo-Christian axis discovered this new vision of man in function of its belief in the one transcendent God of heaven and earth. A truly transcendent God meant that all men were summoned to a life of personalized and individuated existence. Transcending cultural pluralism was, then, built into the Judaeo-Christian faith. An early prayer of Nicholas of Cusa expressed this notion rather well:

It is Thou, O God, who art being sought in the various religions in various ways, and named with various names,

128

for Thou remainest as Thou art, to all incomprehensible
and inexpressible. Be gracious and show Thy counte-
nance. . . . When Thou wilt graciously perform it, then
the sword, jealous hatred, and all evil will cease and all
will come to know that there is but *one* religion in the variety of religious customs.[2]

For the early Christians, the new vision of humanity had been
confirmed by Jesus and was felt to be final. As Tertullian
expressed it: "Nos sumus in quos decurerrunt fines saecu-
lorum" ("We are those upon whom the ends of the ages have
come").[3] The essential lesson had already been learned. All
that remained was for others to come to the new level of understanding that had already been revealed. Yet, as I hope to show
now, this first Judaeo-Christian effort to transcend cultural
pluralism was necessarily too naive. Formulated, as it was, in
an age unaware of the historical relativity of truth, it inhibited
the appreciation that Christianity, too, would have more les-
sons to learn.

Basically, certain key factors are calling into question the
adequacy of the axial period's answers to pluralism, and, in
particular, Christianity's answer. The first key factor is the one
essayed in our last chapter—namely, historical consciousness.
It was this that prompted Ernst Troeltsch to write his famous
work *The Absoluteness of Christianity and the History of Religion* in 1901, and it is this same factor which Bernard Loner-
gan sees as the key in Christianity's ability to give a positive
assessment to the various world religions.[4]

As Christians become increasingly historically conscious,
the problem of religious pluralism will have to be faced anew.
For one thing, historical consciousness simply means that the
reality of religious pluralism is experienced in a qualitatively
new way by contemporary Christians. For whereas previously
Christians entered into an inter-religious dialogue without an
awareness of their own historically- and culturally-conditioned
beliefs, today this historical naiveté has broken down. Consider, for example, the important declaration from the Catholic
side at Vatican II: "Therefore, if the influence of events or of
the times has led to deficiencies in conduct, in Church dis-

cipline, or even in the formulation of doctrine (which must be carefully distinguished from the deposit itself of faith), these must be appropriately rectified at the proper moment."[5] To be sure, this is not a conciliar endorsement of religious relativism. Yet it does manifest a sensitivity to the historically conditioned nature of the religious quest. As this sensitivity grows, it will mean that an interreligious dialogue will no longer simply be a matter of discussing secondary points of difference within an already established, immutable, and a-historical set of Christian presuppositions. The possibility emerges of viewing those very presuppositions as historically conditioned. Charles Davis seems to have this in mind when he queries whether "the event and message of Christ is relevant in its very meaning to forms of the human religious quest outside the Semitic and Western tradition."[6] That is, perhaps the historical nature of Christianity means that Christians should consider whether their very conception of the religious quest is not tied to their own historically-conditioned development. Wilfred Cantwell Smith has made a similar observation:

> One of the facile fallacies that students of comparative religion must early learn to outgrow is, we have felt, the supposition that the different religions give differing answers to essentially the same questions. We would hold that rather their distinctiveness lies in considerable part in a tendency to ask different questions.[7]

Second, an historical consciousness brings the reality and contribution of the world religions and other non-religious world views into greater prominence in the Christian mind. For an historically conscious religion no longer views itself as a "complete" manifestation of man's religious spirit. In this regard, Vatican II's *Declaration on the Relationship of the Church to Non-Christian Religions,"* in stating that the latter "often reflect a ray of that truth which enlightens all men," but which the *Church* proclaims in Christ, is unsatisfactory.[8] The implication is too easily drawn that the Church's proclamation itself is complete and raised beyond history. Yet, once history is taken seriously as a medium of saving truth, then the possibility opens up, not only of religions expressing similar insights into religious wisdom under the influence of their respective historical experiences, but of some religions expressing those insights more fully and powerfully than others. For example, a case could be made that the Reformers gave expression to the transcendent element in Christianity in a more effective manner than did Roman Catholicism during the Reformation period. Similarly, perhaps the Free Churches' critique of both Catholicism's and Protestantism's "institutional view" of Christianity gave unique expression to the fundamental insight that the religious quest transcends institutional boundaries, an insight made possible by their own unique religious history. Further, a case could be made that some of the world's high religions witness to religious values that at least remain dormant if not even reflectively grasped by the religions of the West.[9] One need only think of how Buddhism's more intuitive and mystical tradition has sensitized its adherents to elements of the religious quest that the West has yet to understand. In this light it seems too facile to say that the West's current interest in the meditative wisdom and techniques of the East is simply a fad. Rather, a good case could be made that the Western experience, under the influence especially of technology, has given expression to a more didactic and rationalistic form of the religious quest, while the East has fostered a more intuitive and suprarational approach. Likewise it has recently been suggested that Judaism's rejection of Christianity stems not simply from Jewish inadequacies, but from those, rather, of Christianity itself.[10] That is, a factor of the Jewish rejection is the historical limitations of Christianity itself. In each case, what is at work here is human historicity. The religions have been "shaped" by their historical experiences, and this is not simply or only a limitation, but the medium by which each religion is sensitized to the multiple dimensions of the religious quest.

Third, an historical consciousness makes possible, for the first time, a real dialogue between the religions. For one thing, an historically conscious religion is in the position of really understanding the religious wisdom of the various religions. It is no accident that works like John Dunne's *The Way of All the*

Earth and Thomas Merton's *Mystics and Zen Masters* are appearing for the first time in our age. One might think that the qualitatively new manner in which religious pluralism is experienced today—spoken of above—might render any dialogue futile. For if there is no overreaching and agreed upon set of presuppositions within which to dialogue, how can such an intercommunication ensue? But what this experience proves is that the dialogue is simply much more demanding than previous ages thought, not that it is impossible. For what must not be overlooked is that an historically conscious individual is in a position to grasp the historical contexts that give rise to religious wisdom, and thus in a position to perspectivize religious claims. As Edward Carr once put it: "The historian who is most conscious of his own situation is also more capable of transcending it, and more capable of appreciating the essential nature of the differences between his own society and outlook and those of other periods and other countries."[11]

An historical consciousness, then, by making us recognize our own limited perspective, frees us for real dialogue and mutual understanding. An interesting example of this is provided by Charles Davis.[12] He speaks of a Western tendency, stemming from the Western experience of relativism, heavily empirical and rational, to see in the Hindu religion a similar relativism or religious indifference. But scholars' increasing sensitivities to our different historical experiences have enabled us to grasp that Hindu relativism is quite distinct from that of the West. As Robert Slater explains it:

> Generally speaking, our Western relativism is cold, as cold as the science which sponsors it. It is dispassionate. But the mood of Hindu relativism is different. The breath of it is hot and scorching. It is passionately religious. It is affirmative rather than negative.[13]

In other words, our awareness of the Hindu historical experience has freed us to grasp that its "relativism" stems from a profound sense of the "inexpressibility" of the "One" ("the real is One; the learned call it by various names"), not from a Western religious indifferentism.

Perhaps the best overview of how an historical consciousness has progressively freed us for real dialogue has come from
the learned Friedrich Heiler.[14] In a rather illuminating manner
he illustrates, only rarely without sufficient nuance, how the
historical study of religions has led Christian scholars progressively from, first, an awareness of simply the wealth of the
world's religions, to an "esteem" for them, and then finally to
an acknowledgement of the falsity of many Christian judg-
ments about them. An example of the latter would be the common claim that love of the enemy is unique to Jesus. Here is
Heiler's comment:

> All high religions of the earth, not only the Eastern reli-
> gions of redemption but the pre-Christian religions of the
> West, know the commandment to love the enemy. And the
> Chinese *Li-ki* (Book of Ceremonies) says, "By returning
> hatred with goodness, human concern is exercised toward
> one's own person." The wise Lao-tse emphatically de-
> mands the "reply to adversity with mercy and goodness."
> Loving the enemy has been commanded in India since the
> earliest times. We read in the heroic epic Mahābhārata:
> "Even an enemy must be afforded appropriate hospitality
> when he enters the house; a tree does not withhold its
> shade even from those who come to cut it down."[15]

When one remembers that the Christian Tertullian asserted
that loving the enemy was an exclusively Christian claim, one
begins to grasp how historical consciousness is freeing him to
enter into genuine dialogue.[16]

In addition, an historically conscious dialogue not only
fosters communication, it fosters change. For if one remembers
that human historicity means that man develops and alters
himself and his institutions, then one can begin to see that any
genuine increment in understanding can effect a proportionate
change in man himself. As history indicates, knowledge is
never simply the contemplation of what is, but also brings
about what can be. The implications this carries for the in-
traworld dialogue cannot yet be predicted. Of necessity, that
dialogue, until now, has been "past-oriented," concentrated

around simply attempting to grasp the religious wisdom present in the various religions. But an awareness of the "transforming" nature of knowledge would seem to indicate that the dialogue will increasingly take on a "futuristic" orientation, leading perhaps to the discovery of religious values and religious styles of life hitherto unsuspected. Avery Dulles has alluded to the same phenomenon occurring among Christians: "To the extent that believers of different confessions share a similar commitment to the values of justice, peace, freedom, and fraternal love, they find themselves drawn together into a community of action that transcends their present denominational barriers and paves the way for a richer unity in faith and worship."[17] Dialogue creates a different sort of person, as a Thomas Merton illustrates rather well.

Thus, an historical consciousness has given a new shape to the experience of pluralism. For the Christian, at least, it is creating a widened, more pluralistic style of awareness. Ever since the Renaissance, with its quest for discovery, this expansion of the Christian mind has been progressively taking shape. But what is also important to notice is that this historical consciousness has gone hand in hand with the second key factor giving a new shape to the experience of human pluralism. We have in mind the phenomenon variously known as "world unification," "planetization," or even "cosmification." Karl Jaspers has perhaps formulated it most perceptively:

What is historically new and for the first time in history decisive about our situation is the real unity of mankind on the earth. The planet has become for man a single whole dominated by the technology of communication; it is "smaller" than the Roman Empire was formerly.[18]

While our first factor—historical consciousness—seems to highlight the positive features of the new shape of religious pluralism, planetization seems, thus far, to bring to the fore its negative features. Simultaneously it emphasizes the urgency of taking seriously the encounter between the world religions and other "world systems of thought." John Dunne sees in this phenomenon the possible emergence of a "collective mind," but he also grasps the actuality of man's failure and perhaps even fear of developing such a mentality. As he expressively states it:

> The world wars, it is true, are the most obvious signs that the transition to world history has been taking place in this century. They have arisen rather from a failure to pass over, and they are massive events beyond the influence of the individual. That the failure to pass over should be so deadly, though, seems to show that the time for passing over is ripe and overripe. As for the massiveness and inevitability of the events, it is perhaps only the massiveness and inevitability that always makes its appearance when a journey of the Spirit is called for and does not occur. There are two ways of going through life, Jung has said. One is to walk through upright and the other is to be dragged through. We could say the same thing of time and history. The transition from history to world history is something man can walk through upright on a journey of the Spirit, or it is something he can be dragged through in a series of world wars.[19]

Jaspers, in line with Dunne, indicates some of the difficulties involved in planetization, and I would like to indicate their relevance to the new world encounter Christianity is undergoing. First, "the masses have become a decisive factor in the historical process," says Jaspers. What he means is that planetary intercommunication entails an exposure to differing historical experiences, world views, and ideological systems of thought. One might almost say an "overexposure." While this *could be* the necessary foundation for a strengthening and enriching of individuals and cultures, it seems instead to result in a lessening of personal and cultural self-identity and integration. Since *all* are exposed to these disruptive forces, the "people" are becoming the "masses." And while, of course, charismatic leaders could do much to stem this, the masses greatly seem to determine the kind of leaders they want. Something similar happens in the normal development of a child, whose varied, pluralistic experiences can eventually lead to an enriching of the personality, but all too often only place the child into greater confusion and inner schizophrenia. Would it be erroneous to suppose that today's complex religious pluralism is fostering a similar shift, from the formerly integrated Christian "people" to the confused, identity-less, and sometimes indifferent Christian "masses"? A fruitful world dialogue would require a high degree of self-possession and identity. Perhaps one of the factors underlying the seeming lack of progress in the ecumenical effort, both between Christians and between Christianity and the world religions, is the existence of the Christian masses, unable to cope with the exceedingly high demands of such an encounter.

Jaspers' second factor could perhaps be called the "universalization of doubt" which has spawned various movements destructive of any progress in the world dialogue. One such movement would be the natural tendency toward "thinking in ideologies," characteristic of "the abasements of psychoanalysis and vulgar Marxism."[20] Such a response is normal in an age of mass confusion and confrontation of world views. It is the perennial response of refusing to really meet the questions, to close in flanks, to retreat into the clear recesses of the ghetto, to legitimate one's refusal to change by ideology. While this has always been a basic human strategy, what is new about it today is its universal and planetary influence:

> But perhaps the formation of ideologies really is particularly great in its compass today. For in hopelessness there arises the need for illusion, in the aridity of personal existence the need for sensation, in powerlessness the need to violate those who are even more powerless.[21]

Jaspers' lapse into ideology would not appear to be an unreal problem for Christianity as it enters into this new planetary age. Perhaps this "ideologizing" in no small measure accounts for much of the aridity in the ecumenical effort. Karl Rahner has recently pointed out that planetization is increasingly transforming Christianity into a "real" religion, one that is no longer adhered to simply because it is the controlling religious institution of the culture. However, as this process continues, Christianity too will face the temptation of ideology as its way of coping with our universal pluralism. As Rahner put it: "If we talk of the 'little flock' to defend our cozy traditionalism and stale pseudo-orthodoxy, in fear of the mentality of modern man and modern society, if we tacitly consent to the departure of restless, questioning people from the Church, so that we can return to our repose and orderly life and everything in the Church becomes as it was before, we are propagating, not the attitude proper to Christ's little flock, but a petty sectarian mentality."[22] The natural outcome of such ideological thinking is, as Jaspers indicates, a tendency toward "simplification," in which easy slogans, simplistic solutions, and the seeking out of scapegoats are thought to be the answer.

Thus, the phenomenon of planetization, while it offers us the possibility of a transcultural enrichment hitherto unknown, at the same time endangers it. The possibilities for the world dialogue opening up through historical consciousness in a sense can be "universalized" through planetization. They can also be thwarted. A most decisive option is placed before us:

> For whereas all previous periods of crucial change were local and susceptible of being supplemented by other happenings in other places, in other worlds, so that even if they failed the possibility of the salvation of man by other movements was left open, what is happening now is absolutely decisive. There is no longer anything outside it.[23]

The World Encounter in the Christian Imagination

The problem of religious pluralism, as the above clearly manifests, has been greatly complexified since the axial period. The ultimate difficulty was the a-historical self-understanding of Judaeo-Christianity. Since the Renaissance and its gradual development of an historical consciousness, Christian theologians have been forced to confront the problem of the world religions, and by way of a propaedeutic to my own approach, I would like to present a survey of the various solutions that have been proposed from the Christian side. Basically these various approaches can be understood as "reflections" of the various stages of Christianity's own growing historical consciousness. As its awareness of human historicity becomes more far-reaching, so, too, do its solutions.

Throughout I will be presuming a basic familiarity with the Christian claims. Similarly I will be limiting my analysis to the encounter between the world religions. Actually, as Paul Tillich especially has pointed out,[24] today's world encounter would also have to embrace other systems of thought, most notably that of the humanism (Tillich calls it "secularism") we essayed in the last chapter. I am not interested here in giving a critique of these various world views. My focus, rather, is upon the attitude in the Christian imagination with which these various world views have been and can be approached.

All of these approaches, in various ways, either do partial justice or no justice at all to the historical nature of man's religious quest. A first, early form of this in Roman Catholicism resulted in the theological attempts, especially prior to Vatican II, to relate the individual non-Christian to Christianity in various "grades" of membership. For example, one could distinguish between the baptism of water and the baptism of desire, a view which won official recognition in Pope Pius XII's *Mystici Corporis* and even in some decrees of the Second Vatican Council.[25] Although this represents an attempt to give a positive assessment of the non-Christian, from the viewpoint of our own analysis it is based on the unhistorical presupposition that "the individual was saved in spite of pagan social environment rather than in any way because of it."[26] This view would make no room for an encounter with the world religions, but only for individuals within those various religions. Ultimately it betrays an insensitivity to man's historical nature, which may explain why it was the common Roman Catholic approach to this question. Protestant thinkers, who faced up to the problems posed for Christianity by historical consciousness much earlier than Catholic thinkers in general, have more commonly dealt with the question of the encounter of the religions. The Second Vatican Council, in its *Decree on the Relationship of the Church to Non-Christian Religions*, has shown a new sensitivity to the positive role of the various religions. Further, our own analysis throughout has sought to show how the great breakthroughs in human development are unintelligible without the positive role that one's historical and social context has played.

What has been called the "dialectical" approach among Protestants is closely allied to the above position. This view, espoused in its strongest form by Karl Barth and in a mitigated form by Paul Tillich,[27] would try to make room for the non-Christian religions by stressing the oppositional or dialectical relationship between the historical forms of religion and God's one transcendent presence. The latter transcends all boundaries, including Christianity, thus creating a space for the non-Christian religions within God's salvific plan. While this view has the advantage of granting some place to the various religions (and not simply individuals), it is excessively negative toward all actual concrete and historical forms of religion. The positive nature of the latter is not brought out. Again, I think this is the "Catholic" mistake transposed into another form. Ultimately, it too seems to betray an unhistorical view of religion. An historical consciousness, while to some extent critical of the possible conditioning factors of a religion's historicity, would not view the latter in simply a negative light. Rather, a religion's historicity is itself the medium of man's religious experience. It would seem that we can only realistically participate in a genuine encounter of the religions by grasping the positive nature of one another's historical traditions.

While the above approaches grant too little significance to the positive role of religion, another view would grant it too much significance. This would occur when any religion would claim that it is the *fullest* historical expression of man's religious quest. Generally this approach has been espoused by Christians who have maintained that Christianity gives fullest expression to the one religious quest occurring throughout man's history. Rahner's theory of anonymous Christianity has sometimes been seen as a modern rendition of this theory. But even if, as the Christian must, one affirms the Christian claims to superiority, those claims do not exist a-historically, but in the concrete manifestation of Christianity at a particular epoch. Thus, for example, medieval Christianity incarnated its beliefs in the historical form of "Christendom," a medieval synthesis of culture and religion. It would be extremely difficult to maintain that this was the fullest expression of man's religious quest, even in the medieval period. A more historical view would maintain that a religion's historicity both aids and limits the religious quest. Just as today we look back at the medieval synthesis and are aware of its cultural limitations, there is no reason to think that later ages will not appraise the present form of Christianity in a similar way. From the non-Christian side, this view would not grant a real historicity to the various world religions. It would treat the world religions as curious museum pieces which ceased developing centuries ago. Yet, historically, the possibility remains open that these religions have continued to develop and either have or will develop religious values which are as integral to the religious quest as are those expressed by Christianity. Furthermore, in our own planetary culture the possibility of transcultural influence seems more and more likely. What this means is that the various world religions may very well appropriate the religious values expressed in Christianity. What is crucial to note, however, is that it is unhistorical to assume that the only way this could occur is through the acceptance of the historical form of Christianity as we know it now.

A more radical approach to the world encounter, which again stems from a certain approach to the historicity of religion, is the "relativistic" solution. Usually thought to be espoused by Ernst Troeltsch, this would relativize all religious claims, and is commonly known as the "liberal" solution to our problem. In Davis' words: "The religious relativism comes out in various ways: each religion appropriately expresses its own culture; there is not absolute truth in religion, only truth for us; all religions are different paths to the same goal."[28]

First, some preliminary remarks. I have already suggested that the Christian cannot genuinely participate in the new encounter of the religions unless he is willing to grant full significance to the historical (and thus cultural and traditional) elements in the various religions. Now I would suggest that this genuine encounter cannot proceed unless the Christian takes seriously the element of the absolute in the various religions.

The evidence indicates that all the high religions are equally adamant in their acceptance of the absolute. Heiler, for one, has described this well:

Above and beneath the colorful world of phenomena is concealed the "true being" . . . as Plato says; the "reality of all realities," "the one without a counterpart" according to the Upanishad, "the eternal truth" in Islamic Sufism. Above all things transient rises the great cosmos, the eternal order, the *Tao* of ancient China, the ṛtam of ancient India, the Logos of ancient Greece. This reality is constantly personified in religious imagery as Yahweh, Varuna, Ahura Mazdah, Allah, Vishnu, Krishna, Buddha, Kali, Kwan Yin. . . . The personal and rational elements in the concept of God, the "thou" toward God, however, at no time exhaust the fully transcendent divine reality.[29]

It is because the various religions take the element of the absolute so seriously that any genuine encounter will also have to reckon with differences in the various absolute claims. As Davis puts it: "The great religions are beyond pretense in conflict over the nature of the transcendent and over man and his fulfillment."[30]

Most importantly, however, the liberal solution exemplified by Troeltsch is closely tied to the relativistic historicism which gave it birth. Any number of recent theological studies have plausibly pointed out the hidden *a priori* against the absolute involved in that historicism. The position seems to be gaining acceptance among theologians that historicity does not necessarily lead to the denial of the absolute. It rather highlights the long and varied historical road which man travels in pursuit of the absolute. Finally, my entire analysis of human development inevitably leads to the conclusion of the reality of the absolute. I have sought to show that at different stages of development that absolute has been variously understood, and unless one wants to grant no significance to human development, one must reckon seriously with the different perspectives on the absolute which have emerged in the course of the development of human consciousness. From this perspective, the relativistic approach really fails to take human historicity seriously. By granting no real significance to the varied views of the absolute that have emerged in human history, it ultimately underestimates man's progressive maturation in consciousness.[31]

Quite clearly the difficulties with all of the above approaches have to do with their inadequate appropriation of an historical consciousness. Other difficulties could perhaps be pointed out, from a specifically theological or metaphysical perspective, but for our purposes the difficulties which an historical consciousness is able to signalize are sufficient for querying the possibilities of another approach. Recently Charles Davis, fully informed of the difficulties we have pointed out, has clarified the matter somewhat by indicating that it is possible for Christians both to maintain their own convictions and yet still to enter into a genuine dialogue with the non-Christians, a dialogue in which both parties could truly learn. Davis' key point is his contention that "even under the sovereignty of God history is open-ended, offering a manifold of possibilities for actualization by men."[32] This leads Davis to reformulate the function of Christianity as one of representation, "involving both service and redemptive suffering":

> Christians will indeed preach Christ universally. Their witness to Christ, when offered without arrogance, will have many indirect effects, apart from direct conversions. And these direct conversions themselves should be regarded, not as the first steps in gathering all men into the Christian Church as a visible community on earth, but as God's election of some for a special representative role.[33]

I regard Davis' view as a real improvement over previous views. It is fully historically conscious, assigns a positive role to all the religions, and yet maintains a sensitivity to the need for respecting each religion's stance toward the absolute. Further, Davis maintains a self-critical stance: "I see no reason for indiscriminately swallowing all that the various religions offer and every reason for engaging in a careful discussion of the difficult issues they raise."[34] Yet, despite Davis' clear improvement over previous views, I wonder if he has adequately presented the Christian function and task for our times.

What I find most attractive in Davis' view is its appreciation of history as open-ended, offering manifold possibilities of actualization by men. This clearly views history as itself the medium of religious truth. Religious truth is not ready-made and a-historical. Precisely because of this it is not the monopoly of one tradition. My one question has to do with whether Davis' view of Christianity's mission is quite up to his insight into human and religious historicity. By describing Christianity's mission as one of redemptive representation, does he not run the danger of describing a *living* faith in terms of an a-historical mission? The point is that Jesus' redemptive suffering took a particular historical form at a particular epoch. The crucial issue today is: To what historical form of representation do our times summon Christianity?

On the Need for a Transcultural Consciousness

Until now Christian theologians have been principally concerned with the question of whether Christian principles would really admit an authentic encounter of the religions. Our discussion of the various views, additionally confirmed by Davis' own approach, leads us to the conclusion that this encounter is not only possible but demanded by Christian principles themselves. However, I think that our present situation permits us to go further than Davis and give more precision to the actual historical mission to which our times are summoning us.

Let me begin with a clue from Raimundo Panikkar. In a highly engaging article he has spoken of the emergence of a new myth in our times: "the myth of the unity of the family of man in a global human culture which embraces all cultures and religions, so they become mutually enriching and challenging facets of the one total human experience."[35] This myth is equivalent, says Panikkar, to Teilhard de Chardin's need "for a field of sympathy on a planetary scale." But Panikkar indicates that we "still lack a universal horizon, a reference point accepted because it is acceptable, a unifying myth for our times."[36] And he predicts:

> For good or for ill the world is in ferment and foment. The absentees become decisive factors, impelling change. If the venerable traditions of mankind do not collaborate in forging a new consciousness, this latter will emerge without their direct contribution. We can welcome or regret this turn of events, but either way we cannot ignore the urgency of the situation.[37]

Karl Rahner would seem to be echoing Panikkar's intuitions in a recent article on dogma's historical development. Therein he maintains that the history of Christian thought has two great epochs, "that of the process of the attainment of . . . full development" through a history of relating with the world to various degrees, "and that of the global dialogue with the entire unified (which does not mean peacefully reconciled) mind of humanity." However, most importantly, he thinks that the great lesson that Christianity is learning from this experience is to discern that "the message of Christianity is not tied to any particular stage or region of man's self-understanding. This meant that the understanding of the faith had to be detached from the mental horizons of Judaism and Hellenism, to become, as it ought to be, a dialogue with the world."[38] Rahner seems to be arguing that the experience of planetization is deregionalizing the Christian mind, thus enabling it to more clearly distinguish the culturally-limited from the more universally significant features of the Christian faith.

Following Rahner's lead, I think it would be worthwhile to explore whether our present planetary experience might not represent an experience for the Christian that will enable him to grasp perhaps a facet of his faith either unknown or only dimly glimpsed by pre-planetary Christians. I am suggesting that under the influence of its own current experience, Christianity may be undergoing a process of sensitization to certain values that hitherto remained only dimly glimpsed, if glimpsed at all. This process of development through sensitization has happened more than once in Christianity's history. Our previous analysis of Christianity's gradual appropriation of an historical consciousness was an example of this process at work. That development has sensitized Christians to the fact that professing the faith is not a matter of world escapism into another a-worldly realm, but one of appropriating the expanded consciousness necessary for a responsible life in this world. Some further examples might be useful. In grappling with the issues of human historicity and freedom since the Enlightenment, theologians, precisely under the influence of this experience, have been sensitized to features of the Christian message hitherto unclearly known. Thus, whereas previous ages could not grasp the contradiction between the universal commandment of love and the institution of slavery, our age can. Whereas previous ages thought that to admit history's open-endedness would involve a denial of God's providential control of the universe, our age sees little difficulty here. Examples could be multiplied, but what they clearly show is the profound manner in which man's current experience sensitizes him and enables him to grasp aspects of reality hitherto unknown. Interestingly enough, the Second Vatican Council seems to point this out: "The human race is passing through a new stage of its history. . . . Hence we can already speak of a true social and cultural transformation, one which has repercussions on man's religious life as well."[39]

I would propose, then, that our contemporary experience of planetization represents a new experience for Christianity. As Jaspers puts it, what is decisively new is the real unity of man. I would further propose that this new experience is contributing toward a sensitization in the contemporary Christian. One could almost say that a new "universalized" consciousness is being developed, insofar as this new experience is qualitatively altering the contemporary Christian's way of perceiving himself and his faith. And I would further propose that this new experience represents a "plus" for Christianity, insofar as it seems to be the catalyst for a more profound understanding of the faith.

First, then, our contemporary experience of planetization, while it is the cause of great world disorder and religious and political ideology, is also the basis for a fundamental maturing of the contemporary Christian consciousness. Certain forerunners, in whom I would say the experience of planetization has been healthily integrated, have indicated the general features of this new consciousness. The rest of us, unfortunately, would seem to be in a "twilight" stage: the contours of what we are experiencing are neither black as at night nor white and clear as during the day; they are rich in possibilities, but obscure and confusing, the multifaceted richness blocking us from a clear perception of what might eventually ensue.

One such forerunner, whose insights I will endeavor to develop in the terms used throughout this book, is Thomas Merton. In a highly suggestive essay, in part inspired by the Persian psychoanalyst Reza Arasteh, he has developed the notion of a "transcultural consciousness."[40] Arasteh's notion of "final integration," developed from the prior insights of Erich Fromm, Viktor Frankl, and Persian Sufism, led Merton to his own valuable insights. This "final integration" is not the "cure" of psychic sickness resulting from adaptation to society. Arasteh is quite critical of that limited notion of "cure": "Dr. Arasteh is interested not only in the partial and limited 'health' which results from contented acceptance of a useful role in society, but in the final and complete maturing of the human psyche on a transcultural level."[41]

Cultural adaptation, in Arasteh's view, does not really cure illness, but only provides a way of living with it. Merton adds that a real cure is especially inhibited if the society to which one adapts is "unhealthy because of its overemphasis on cerebral, competitive, acquisitive forms of ego-affirmation."[42] The problem is especially exacerbated when the techniques of cure—therapy, psychoanalysis, religion, etc.—are drafted into the service of "adapting" the individual to his society or to some organization within that society. Then people think they are healthy when in fact they are really ill. In this situation, not only is "illness" fostered; it is preferred.

A further point made by Arasteh is the distinction between anxiety which stems from the individual who has surrendered to mere cultural adaptation and thus blocked his own potential growth, and that stemming from the individual who experiences the incompleteness of such a "cure." The latter anxiety "is a sign of health and generates the necessary strength for psychic rebirth into a new transcultural identity."[43] This identity is one in which the individual has recaptured his creativity and uniqueness, thus transcending the limitations of society and prejudice.

Merton's description of this new, transcultural identity is somewhat lyrical, yet nonetheless convincing:

Final integration is a state of transcultural maturity far beyond mere social adjustment, which always implies partiality and compromise. . . . He apprehends his life fully and wholly from an inner ground that is at once more universal than the empirical ego and yet entirely his own He is in a certain sense "cosmic" and "universal man."

The man who has attained final integration is no longer limited by the culture in which he has grown up. . . . He accepts not only his own community, his own society, his own friends, his own culture, but all mankind. He does not remain bound to one limited set of values in such a way that he opposes them aggressively or defensively to others. He is fully "Catholic" in the best sense of the word. He has a unified vision and experience of the one truth shining out in all its various manifestations, some clearer than others, some more definite and more certain than others. He does not set these partial views up in opposition to each other, but unifies them in a dialectic or an insight of complementarity. . . . With this view of life he is able to bring perspective, liberty and spontaneity into the lives of others.[44]

Could it be that our contemporary planetary experience is generating such a transcultural identity? The anxiety is clearly present: Dunne's world wars, Jaspers' masses and ideologies. In part this anxiety stems from a refusal to break through to a new transcultural level, from a capitulation to mere cultural adaptation. However, Merton's vision gives us hope that a new and more complete transcultural identity may be in the making. Interestingly enough, planetization does seem to foster cultural adaptation. Insofar as it fosters man's experience of confusion and loss of a secure identity, it compels him to seek for some kind of resolution, however simplistic. On the other hand, if worked through, planetization could lead to that fuller identity which Merton envisions.[45] In fact, in a really unified world like our own, mere cultural adaptation will be increasingly experienced as inadequate. This breakdown of cultural adaptation might be a necessary condition for the breakthrough to a deepened transcultural identity.

At this point I should perhaps add that Merton's "transcultural personality" is no mere syncretistic mind. The transcultural person does not "swallow" everything, but is in possession of that inner freedom and detachment that enables him to perspectivize, appreciate, discern, and at times rebel. Further, it would be a mistake to understand the transcultural person in a quantitative manner, as if he knew all the values inherent in any culture. Merton seems to be speaking qualitatively, and has in mind the emergence of a man of sufficient inner calm and personal and cultural detachment that he is capable of recognizing the genuine values present in every person and every culture. In this sense, Merton's transcultural person is fundamentally different from the Renaissance image of the "universal man," who supposedly knew everything there is to know. In fact, as human knowledge complexifies, as it certainly is in our times, the Renaissance image seems more and more "incredible."

Is Merton's vision really a possibility? In terms of the analysis used throughout this entire work, the emergence of a transcultural consciousness would not be a wholly unparalleled event. I have tried to maintain throughout that the "breakthroughs" in history have developed from intensifications of elements previously present in human consciousness. Axial consciousness developed from and intensified the rationality present in and called for by the era of the great civilizations. Historical self-consciousness developed from and intensified the axial sense of individuation. Surprisingly enough, I would suggest that a transcultural individual would be someone who has developed an even more refined sense of individuation. I am taking my clue for this notion from Jung:

> [The development of the person to full ripeness] is at once a charism and curse because its first fruit is the conscious and unavoidable segregation of the individual from the undifferentiated and unconscious herd. This means isolation, and there is no more comforting word for it. Neither family nor society nor position can save him from the fate, nor yet the most successful adaptation to his environment.[46]

In other words, involved in the experience of individuation, when it is developed far enough, is the breakdown of all partial views of the self. The self is not identical with family, society, position, or culture. As Merton indicates, the person then "apprehends his life fully and wholly from an inner ground that is at once more universal than the empirical ego and yet entirely his own." This new apprehension leads to a more liberated self, a self freed from the partial, the cultural, the social. This does not mean that the individual necessarily rejects any of these; it only means that he recognizes them as partial elements co-constituting him as the individual that he is. A transcultural consciousness, then, would be one with a heightened and intensified awareness of this "liberated self." Additionally, Merton maintains that this transcultural person is precisely what Christian belief itself should lead to. In his words:

> For a Christian, a transcultural integration is eschatological. The rebirth of man and of society on a transcultural level is a rebirth into the transformed and redeemed time, the time of the Kingdom, the time of the Spirit, the time of "the end." It means a disintegration of the social and cultural self, the product of merely human history, and the reintegration of that self in Christ, in salvation history, in the mystery of redemption, in the Pentecostal "new creation."[47]

In terms of human consciousness—the perspective of our study—what Merton is really describing is the fully individuated and post-conventional Christian of the axial period. We recall that simultaneous with the discovery of one's autonomy is the discovery of one's freedom. The individuated "I" knows he is more than a simple reflection of societal and cultural values. It is this element of autonomous freedom that Merton is accentuating. The truly autonomous Christian has simply developed his individuation "to full ripeness" and thereby discovered his real freedom from every partial aspect of the self: family, society, position, or culture. He can thereby transcend the cultural, perspectivize it, and appreciate its true but limited worth. Merton refers to this as a "freedom in the spirit," a "liberation from the limits of all that is merely partial and fragmentary in a given culture."[48] This point is very important. It again returns us to the notion that because the Judaeo-Christian defines his identity in terms of a transcendent source, the Christian's autonomy and freedom should be truly transcendent. In his highly creative way, Merton has provided us with a view which illuminates the transcultural possibilities implied in the Judaeo-Christian notion of individuation. In this way we are enabled to understand that the transcultural individual does not annul the breakthrough to individuality that was initiated by the Judaeo-Christian axis, but he rather complexifies it and brings it to a greater completion.

If this interpretation is correct, then the planetary experience of our times could lead to a real completion of what was begun in the axial period. Our planetary experience could be the necessary condition for the eventual development of a truly Christian transcultural consciousness. Should such a consciousness ever achieve the dominance that rationality did in the axial period, we might see the crossing of a new threshold in human history. Like our other breakthroughs, this would not be an annulment of the previous phases of human development, but their further complexification and completion. It completes the axial and historical awareness of individuation by developing that individuation to "full ripeness." By breaking down every "partial" view of the self, it creates an inner space enabling the person to perspectivize, transcend, and appreciate everything partial, without being dominated by it. By freeing him from partiality, it creates an inner space for other "I's."

Thus I think that our planetary experience could lead to a recapturing and intensifying of the transculturalizing possibilities of Christian individuation. The freedom from all personal and cultural partiality and compromise which this promises could lead to a deepened sense of what it truly means to be "Catholic." We are not referring, of course, to the limited sense which the word carries when "being Catholic" is identified with a partial, cultural manner of living the Catholic faith. That interpretation of "Catholic" was normal enough when Christianity aligned itself with the Western culture from the time of Constantine on. The kind of Catholic we have in mind is one who "does not remain bound to one limited set of values in such a way that he opposes them aggressively or defensively to others." But neither does this Catholic swallow anything that any religion or system of thought has to offer. He recognizes the partiality of every view, not setting them up in opposition to each other, but, as Merton indicates, unifying "them in a dialectic or an insight of complementarity." From a traditional theological viewpoint, this perhaps enables us to understand why Christian belief maintains the notion of the communion of saints. Insofar as that belief fosters final integration and transcultural appreciation, it entails a belief in that suppression of all partiality and compromise characterized by the communion of saints.[49]

What must not be overlooked, however, is that Christians cannot create a transcultural consciousness simply by fiat. It would be a fatal mistake for Christians to notionally think that their belief fosters a transcultural mentality, and then to continue on with their narrow and provincial lives. If our historical consciousness has taught us anything, it is that man truly learns and transforms himself from his actual historical experience. A child's consciousness is narrow and partial because his experience is narrow and partial. As Dunne likes to point out, the child lives "on the level of the here and now." If what counts as an ultimate value for a child is immediate gratification, it is not because he is evil, but because his experience is largely limited to the immediate. Similarly the youth's consciousness is only slightly less partial and narrow, not because he too is simply egocentric, but because his experience has not yet widened to the point of being able to grasp values which transcend his very own self. The key is experience, and the desire to both widen and learn from that experience. Likewise, Merton's transcultural Christian must acually engage himself in the sorts of experiences that will facilitate his transcending of cultural partiality. It is no accident that Merton made his own inner passage to the wisdom of the East as well as the wisdom of many other systems of thought. It was in that "passage" that he discovered that deeper, more whole self which transcends partiality. A similar passage is being required of us in this planetary age, and only by endeavoring to make it can we discover our own, more whole selves. Dunne put this well: "To the extent that man ... welcomes the mutual understanding that comes about by passing over, to that extent it does seem, at this time, that he is headed toward some kind of collective consciousness."[50]

We Christians are now in the midst of a transculturalizing process. The two world wars are perhaps its most dramatic negative manifestation. Its manifestation in the Christian churches is the breakdown of "Christendom," the slow and painful detachment from a church of simply a Western and European culture. Rahner has perceptively noticed this:

> The often lamented decline of Christian ways and faith is not the work or effect of sinister forces nor even primarily a decline of really necessary, saving faith. . . . It is simply the disappearance of the pre-condition of that very special kind of faith and Christianity, by no means identical with the essence of faith and Christianity, which was involved in social conditions which are now disappearing.[51]

In other words, Christianity is being transculturalized, and this in direct proportion to its ability to detach itself from a simple identification between "Christendom" and "Christianity." What merits emphasizing is the word "detachment." Just as we cannot create a transcultural consciousness by mere *fiat,* so we cannot do so without great cost to ourselves. Merton indicated that a sign within the individual of the passage from simply cultural adaptation to final transcultural integration is anxiety.

So, too, then, we should expect a similar anxiety to manifest itself in the Church as a whole, throughout this difficult process
of detachment.[52] This process must include, first, a detachment
from the sociological phenomenon of Christendom, and its
identification of the Western culture with Christianity. With
this goes an inevitable tendency to stress Western cultural stability and an inherited form of faith at the expense of the kind
of transformation required by our planetary situation. There
must be detachment, secondly, from a conception of the faith
which simply stresses unanimity of thought and expression,
meaning by this the inherited forms of Christendom. Finally,
there must be detachment from our all too natural defense
mechanisms, in the face of the development we are being asked
to undergo: the feeling of being threatened by our ecclesial situation, the yearning for the better times prior to Vatican II, the
desire for certitude at the expense of a serious dialogue with the
world, intolerance, etc.[53] This type of detachment will both call
for and foster the transcultural consciousness we have been endeavoring to describe.

Some Concluding Observations on the
Future Course of Human Consciousness

If the above analysis is correct, we can hope for the emergence of a quite different form of human consciousness, one
which enables us "to keep our identity" and yet rids us "of our
peculiarities, i.e., those provincialisms which make us unfit for
the total human experience."[54] Erich Neumann has made a
similar prediction:

The collapse of the old civilization, and its reconstruction
on a lower level to begin with, will justify themselves because the new basis will have been immensely broadened.
The civilization that is about to be born will be a human
civilization in a far higher sense than any has ever been
before, as it will have overcome important social, national,
and racial limitations. These are not fantastic pipe
dreams, but hard facts, and their birth pangs will bring in-

finite suffering upon infinite numbers of men. Spiritually, politically, and economically our world is an indivisible whole. By this standard the Napoleonic wars were minor *coups d'état,* and the world view of that age, in which anything outside Europe had hardly begun to appear, is almost inconceivable to us in its narrowness.[55]

But furthermore, since man's consciousness determines what man can imagine as a genuine possibility, I think we can further expect that the transcultural individual will increasingly understand the religious values of his faith in a transcultural manner, thus regaining in a more complexified manner his own faith. As Panikkar graphically expressed it, as we "eat thousands of different things, each of different composition . . . all will eventually be converted into [our] own proper proteins."[56] In other words, a transcultural increment in man's imagination could lead to a discovery of the transcultural implications of man's religious values themselves. I do not know what precise form this would take, but I do not think Herbert Richardson is far off the mark in his observation that we can expect a religious "consciousness . . . able to bear a greater multiplicity in unity."[57] Somehow man's religious values would be able to give expression to this multiplicity in unity, in which unity as well as diversity is maximized. From the Christian side perhaps this would mean a more complexified understanding of belief in a transcendent God. After all, a transcendent God really must transcend cultural boundaries. But while this has always been implied in Judaeo-Christian belief, perhaps only now is man's consciousness sufficiently developed to really understand what this means. For a transcultural Christian would really grasp that only as he strives to transcend all personal and cultural partiality and compromise can he authentically witness to his belief in such a God.[58] Additionally, the many recent theological attempts to give greater prominence to the risen Christ— Chardin's Pauline "cosmic Christ," Rahner's "anonymous Christ," Panikkar's "unknown Christ of Hinduism"—would seem to be manifestations of our new transcultural understanding of religious values. Since Christ, for Christians, is the central issue in Christianity, these various transcultural views of Christ illustrate to what extent Christian belief itself is being transculturalized. Each of these interpretations of Christ is attempting to say that Christ, in his risen life, participates in God's own radical transcendence, in the divine ability to transcend cultural boundaries and partiality. This can be seen as a new form of Christian imperialism, a sort of projection onto Christ of Christianity's imperial aspirations. Indeed, for a Christian lacking a transcultural consciousness, this would be a real possibility. But it can also be a manifestation of the promised transculturalizing of Christian belief that we have in mind, a recognition that the Christian's goal is that suppression of all cultural partiality that now characterizes Christ in his risen existence. A really transcultural understanding of Christ would, after all, presuppose a transcultural consciousness in the Christian.[59]

Finally, since each new development in man's consciousness represents a complexification in which the previous gains of consciousness are not annulled but integrated into a greater synthesis, our new transcultural consciousness would not lead to the rejection of the authentic religious values of the past. With Richardson, I would "anticipate the universalization and ratification of the values . . . we have seen emerging."[60]

Notes

1. Weil, *art. cit.*, 29. In my "The Risen Christ, Transcultural Consciousness, and the Encounter of the World Religions," *Theological Studies* 37 (1976) 381-409, I have proposed an analysis similiar to the one found here.

2. As cited by Heiler, *op. cit.*, pp. 154-155.

3. For some early Christian attitudes toward pluralism, see Jaroslav Pelikan, *The Finality of Jesus Christ in an Age of Universal History* (Richmond, 1965). Tertullian's statement is cited on p. 7.

4. Cf. his "The Future of Christianity," lecture given at Holy Cross College, 1969. The flavor of his view can be gleaned from the following: "While classicist culture conceived itself normatively and abstractly, modern culture conceives itself empirically and concretely. It is the culture that recognizes cultural variation, difference, development, breakdown, that investigates each of the many cultures of mankind, that studies their histories, that seeks to understand what the classicist would tend to write off as strange or uncultivated or barbaric. Instead of thinking of man in terms of a nature common to all men whether awake or asleep, geniuses or morons, saints or

sinners [i.e., the axial solution to pluralism], it attends to men in their concrete living. If it can discern common and invariant structures in human operations, it refuses to take flight from the particular to the universal, and it endeavors to meet the challenge of knowing people in all their diversity and mutability."

5. W. M. Abbott, ed., *The Documents of Vatican II* (New York, 1966), p. 350. By only admitting the historically-conditioned nature of doctrinal *formulations* rather than doctrinal *understanding,* the Council only partly manifested an historical consciousness. Still, this was an advance over Trent, for example, which spoke only of "restoration," not "innovation": ". . . in confirmandis dogmatibus et in instaurandis in ecclesia moribus" (G. Alberigo *et al.,* eds., *Conciliorum oecumenicorum decreta* [Rome, 1962], p. 640). Cf. John W. O'Malley, "Reform, Historical Consciousness, and Vatican II's Aggiornamento," *Theological Studies* 32 (1971) 573-601, for Rome's progressive entry into historical awareness.

6. Charles Davis, *Christ and the World Religions* (London, 1970), p. 59.

7. As cited by Davis, *ibid.*

8. Abbott, *op. cit.,* p. 662.

9. A thesis advanced some time ago by F. S. C. Northrop, *The Meeting of East and West: An Inquiry Concerning World Understanding* (New York, 1946/1974), and recently reaffirmed by William Johnston, *Christian Zen* (New York, 1971), p. 29: "But would it be an oversimplification to say that the East has stressed unity and that the West has stressed diversity? And that they need one another? Or, better, to say that the mystic East teaches us in a striking way that all is one, while the scientific West has brilliantly grasped the diversity and the many?" Also, Raimundo Panikkar, "The Emerging Myth," *Monchanin* 8 (1975) 10, interestingly says: "It is an undeniable fact that a good part of contemporary youth is irresistibly attracted to Oriental spiritualities. Many sociologists have studied the problem and have tried to discover the causes for this attraction. And yet this is only one side of the coin. In fact, oriental youth is at least equally fascinated by the life styles, the 'spiritualities' and 'religions' of the West. There are surely more fervent students of Western technology in Asia than there are practitioners of Oriental meditation in the West. Even if we recognize that most of these Easterners turn to Western technology in order to survive, in order to secure the most elementary needs of life, this interest in the West remains nonetheless the way to liberation—much as the spiritual paths of the East are liberating for young Westerners. Moreover, an exogenous dynamism seems to characterize this two-way traffic—we could almost say a law of exogamy. You try to marry outside your own tradition. It is all very well for zealous preachers to insist that we (Westerners, Christians, Hindus, Japanese, Russians, etc.) have in our own tradition what we pursue elsewhere, but they preach in a vacuum . . . because the peoples of the world tend to look *outside* for a solution, a complementarity, a way, a savior, a salvation. But a great wind is blowing across all the boundaries, bearing with it the seeds of dialogue and genuine tolerance."

10. Cf. Rosemary Ruether, *Faith and Fratricide* (New York, 1974).

11. Edward Hallett Carr, *What Is History?* (New York, 1961), pp. 53-54.

12. Davis, *op. cit.,* pp. 37-39.

13. As cited by Davis, *ibid.,* p. 36.

14. Heiler, *op. cit.,* pp. 132-160.

15. *Ibid.*, p. 147.

16. Cf. Tertullian, *Ad scapulam*, 1: "For all love those who love them; it is peculiar to Christians alone to love those who hate them" (*The Ante-Nicene Fathers*, Vol. 3 [Michigan, 1957], p. 105).

17. Avery Dulles, *Models of the Church* (New York, 1974), p. 145. Cf. also John Macquarrie, *Christian Unity and Christian Diversity* (Philadelphia, 1975), p. 23: "The time has come for the Churches to look out together on the world. It might be surprising how much unity would develop unconsciously through a common response to the challenges of contemporary society."

18. Jaspers, *op. cit.*, p. 126; cf., for this section, pp. 126-228. Also see William Irwin Thompson, *Passages about Earth: An Exploration of the New Planetary Culture* (New York, 1974).

19. Dunne, *op. cit.*, p. 151.

20. Jaspers, *op. cit.*, p. 133.

21. *Ibid.*

22. Karl Rahner, *The Shape of the Church To Come* (New York, 1974), p. 30.

23. Jaspers, *op. cit.*, p. 140.

24. Cf. Paul Tillich, *Christianity and the Encounter of the World Religions* (New York, 1963).

25. Cf. Karl Rahner, "Membership of the Church According to the Teaching of Pius XII's Encyclical 'Mystici Corporis Christi,'" in his *Theological Investigations*, Vol. 2 (Baltimore, 1963), pp. 1-88; out of this grew his notion of the "anonymous Christian," which I think does only partial justice to the religions, revealing an individualistic approach to the question. Cf. Anita Röper, *The Anonymous Christian* (New York, 1966). For a similar "strain" in Vatican II, cf. Abbott, *op. cit.*, pp. 31-37.

26. Cf. Davis, *op. cit.*, p. 42; Abbott, *op. cit.*, pp. 660-668; Heinz Robert Schlette, *Towards a Theology of Religions* (New York, 1966).

27. Cf. Karl Barth, "The Revelation of God as the Abolition of Religion," *Church Dogmatics*, Vol. 1, Part 2 (Edinburgh, 1963), pp. 280-361; Paul Tillich, *op. cit.*, and "The Significance of the History of Religions for the Systematic Theologian," in J. M. Kitagawa, ed., *The History of Religions: Essays on the Problem of Understanding* (Chicago, 1967), pp. 241-255.

28. Davis, *op. cit.*, p. 50.

29. Heiler, *op. cit.*, p. 142.

30. Davis, *op. cit.*, p. 50.

31. Some further problems with relativism were recently pointed out by Roderick Hindery, "Pluralism in Moral Theology: Reconstructing Universal Ethical Pluralism," *Proceedings of the Catholic Theological Society of America* 28 (1973) 78: "Relativism blocks interdisciplinary and intercultural dialogues. As a basic rebuttal of a moral point of view, it leaves force or manipulation as the only alternative for solving political and personal differences. . . . Moreover, relativism excuses individual and group egoism and provides a rationale for social non-involvement and toleration of the status quo. In protection of group interests, industrial peoples can relativize values like health and longevity and say of colonial peoples: 'They like dirt and disease and a short life-span, because it is part of their way of life and always has been.'"

32. Davis, *op. cit.*, p. 129. On pp. 128-129 Davis makes three key points

relative to the issue that Christians can maintain their own convictions, especially about Christ, and yet give a positive assessment to the religions: (1) to presuppose otherwise is to presuppose that God's work in Christ is exclusively carried on by Christianity; (2) "as men are in the present historical order, a pluralistic situation seems best to preserve and promote truth and to ward off corruption"; (3) we cannot assume that the explicit acknowledgment of Christianity is God's goal for mankind.

33. *Ibid.*, p. 130.
34. *Ibid.*
35. Raimundo Panikkar, "The Emerging Myth," *Monchanin* 8 (1975) 8.
36. *Ibid.*, 8-9.
37. *Ibid.*, 11.
38. Karl Rahner, "History of Dogma," *Sacramentum Mundi* 2 (1968) 104.
39. Abbott, *op. cit.*, p. 202.
40. Cf. Thomas Merton, "Final Integration: Toward a 'Monastic Therapy,'" in *Contemplation in a World of Action* (New York, 1973), pp. 219-231. Cf. also Reza Arasteh, *Final Integration in the Adult Personality* (Leiden, 1965).
41. *Ibid.*, p. 222.
42. *Ibid.*
43. *Ibid.*
44. *Ibid.*, pp. 225-226.
45. Dunne, *op. cit.*, pp. 153-154, envisions something similar in his notion of a "collective mind."
46. As cited by Merton, *op. cit.*, p. 228.
47. *Ibid.*, pp. 229-230.
48. *Ibid.*, p. 226. According to Merton this Christian freedom enables the person to be "in a certain sense identified with everybody: or in the familiar language of the New Testament . . . he is 'all things to all men.' He is able to experience their joys and sufferings as his own, without however becoming dominated by them. He has attained to a deep inner freedom—the freedom of the Spirit we read of in the New Testament. He is guided not just by will and reason, but by 'spontaneous behavior subject to dynamic insight.' Now, this calls to mind the theology of St. Thomas on the gifts of the Holy Spirit which move a man to act 'in a superhuman mode'" (p. 225). Cf. Rom. 8:35-39.
49. Such might be a transcultural interpretation of this belief which, so far as I can tell, does justice to the data involved. Cf. Stephen Benko, *The Meaning of Sanctorum Communio* (London, 1964).
50. Dunne, *op. cit.*, p. 154.
51. Rahner, *The Shape of the Church To Come, op. cit.*, pp. 24-25.
52. For an interesting analysis of the role of detachment in our planetary culture, see Wilfrid Desan, *The Planetary Man* (New York, 1972), pp. 143-151.
53. See Juan Luis Segundo, *The Community Called Church* (New York, 1973), pp. 44-49, for a development of these insights.
54. Raimundo Panikkar, "Cross-Cultural Studies: The Need for a New Science of Interpretation," *Monchanin* 8 (1975) 12.
55. Neumann, *op. cit.*, p. 393.

56. Raimundo Panikkar, "Religious Education in an Inter-Faith Perspective," *Monchanin* 8 (1975) 32.

57. Richardson, *op. cit.,* p. 137. I am applying Richardson's observations on human consciousness in general to the religious sphere in particular. I would view his "polyconsciousness" as roughly equivalent to my "transcultural consciousness."

58. Cf. Panikkar, "Cross-Cultural Studies: The Need for a New Science of Interpretation," *art. cit.,* 14-15: "'Do you believe in God or don't you?' Here the dialectical method allows no escape: either/or. But what if a particular culture does not put the question in this way? The question simply does not make sense when the God/no God schema is absent (rightly or wrongly) from a world view. Must we answer any question whatsoever, just in order to appease another's dialectical hunger, which in fact merely sheathes a fundamentally narcissistic position and does not contribute positively to our understanding of a different culture?"

59. In my "The Risen Christ, Transcultural Consciousness, and the Encounter of the World Religions," cited earlier, I try to show how this transcultural interpretation of the risen Christ might be further explained and legitimated.

60. Richardson, *op. cit.,* p. 138.

PART IV
SOME
FURTHER PROBINGS

VIII
An Overview: Revelation and Human Development in Consciousness

I suggested earlier that the kind of analysis in which we have been engaged raises questions of a larger metaphysical and theological nature. For example, the Hebraic understanding of a transcendent God raises the issue about the reality of the transcendent. Is the transcendent "God" simply a creation of the Hebraic mind, or is it a reality with which man really has to deal. Similarly, the emergence of the Christian consciousness implies questions about the reality of Jesus which later Christianity was compelled to explore, and which eventually led to the notion of Jesus' divinity, as well as to notions about his personal being (viz., "the hypostatic union"). My desire in this chapter will be to explore the possible clarification which our analysis might contribute to one rather foundational question in Christian theology. The issue which I have in mind is that of the nature of revelation itself. My reason for doing so is that our entire analysis leads in the direction of a reformulation of the nature of revelation. "Revelation," as a category of Christian theology, purports to deal, not simply with God, but with the God-who-manifests-himself-to-man. To employ a category of Gordon Kaufman, revelation concerns "the available God," not God in the fullness of his reality.[1] As such, revelation really concerns the question of God as that God impinges on human consciousness. Whatever else revelation may mean, it at least affirms a human consciousness capable of receiving a divine revelation. If this were consistently thought through, it might clarify some of the questions still debated in theology about the nature of revelation: "There is no consensus among Christian or Catholic theologians as to the forms in which revelation comes, where it is principally found, or how it is related to faith."[2] I am convinced that an

163

analysis of revelation from the perspective of the development of human consciousness can shed decisive light upon each of these debated questions. Further, although the analysis we propose would neither prove nor disprove the reality of a God who communicates himself to man, our analysis might at least indicate what is intended by such an assertion, and thus clarify what is the objective of "proving" in the first place.

SOME THESES REGARDING THE NATURE OF REVELATION

Thesis #1: Corresponding to every view of revelation is a capacity of human consciousness which determines the signification which "revelation" carries.

The purpose of this thesis is to suggest an hypothesis from which, hopefully, we will be able to draw conclusions regarding the nature of revelation. Gordon Kaufman has hit on the key point: "Until and unless man has the possibility of conceiving what occurs within his world as the work of power(s) transcending his experience, he will not be able to conceive either of God(s) or of divine revelation."[3] In other words, Kaufman is pointing to a central thesis of our own book: "revelation" in the Judaeo-Christian sense is directly dependent upon the emergence of a human consciousness capable of grasping the existence and meaning of a transcendent God. From our own perspective this makes very good sense. We have tried to maintain throughout that the level of development of human consciousness determines the horizon of what man can conceive as a genuine possibility. The possibility of a truly transcendent revelation cannot, then, occur for man until his capacities have developed to the point of his being able to distance himself from the immediate and cultural and envisage, through abstraction, a possible transcendent being. The signification of the term "revelation," then, varies directly according to man's corresponding consciousness. In fact, we could go further and maintain that "revelation" is actually a second-order concept used by man to describe what is first and foremost experienced as a development in his own consciousness itself.

This enables us to understand why, historically, "revelation" has carried different meanings, and can be expected to carry still further meanings, as human consciousness develops. As the evidence itself suggests, there exists no *a priori,* a-historical meaning of revelation. Rather, as man's consciousness has developed, so too has his corresponding ability to imagine what really counts as a "revelation" for him. Of course, from a Judaeo-Christian perspective, we can maintain that what actually counts as a "revelation" is the awareness of a transcendent God and the possibilities that such an awareness opens up for man. But this "restriction" of the meaning of revelation was only arrived at after the Hebraic entry into axial consciousness, and, by itself, does not settle the question of whether Judaeo-Christians themselves might not further deepen their awareness of what this "revelation" means as their consciousness develops. The merit, however, of our approach is that it enables us to understand why varying conceptions of revelation have emerged in the course of man's history.

Thesis #2: Each phase of human consciousness generates
its corresponding view of revelation.

This thesis will be explored only schematically, since we are relying upon our previous analyses throughout this book. Just as we viewed the various phases of human consciousness from a high level of abstraction—that is, as ideal types—so our analysis of "revelation" is to be understood in the same way. In reality, we must envisage much more confusion and crossing of boundaries, as the Scriptures themselves even suggest. For example, the constant tension between polytheism and strictly ethical monotheism indicates that the boundaries between the two were somewhat fluid in the Hebraic mind and that the breakthrough to a monotheistic consciousness occurred, at first, only among a certain "elite," such as Jeremiah and his followers. Similarly the tension between Paul and the early Christian Judaizers suggests the same fluidity and partial/incomplete differentiations of consciousness. Remembering these caveats, we might schematize as follows.

(1) Phase One: The Pre-conventional Phase of Human Consciousness

We recall that what characterized this earliest phase of human consciousness was a certain "immediacy" or *participation mystique*. Man dwelled in a sort of undifferentiated immediacy with his environment. The consciousness of being different from nature was not yet developed. This inability to distinguish external reality from subjective thought is what characterized *mythical thinking,* which is why it was so prevalent at this period. The closeness to nature which characterized man at this period led to a veneration of nature as the one real reality with which man has to do. Hence we speak of the "numinous" mentality, in which nature appeared as sacred, that which determined man's fate. Herbert Richardson, whose own studies precipitated this excursion into revelation theology, gives us a good insight into this earliest phase of "revelation":

> The mimetic consciousness of the "tribal" stage makes man regard himself as a subordinate part of his surrounding world. He feels bound to a certain place. He does not, at this stage, think of himself as possessing a life that originates in his own being. Rather, he thinks of the life in himself as infused into him from his total environment. He identifies the breath in his lungs with the wind that blows across his fields.[4]

I would suggest that it was this kind of consciousness which generated what we would today term polytheistic, animistic, and naturalistic views of revelation.

(2) Phase Two: The Conventional Phase of Human Consciousness

We recall that what precipitated this phase of human consciousness was man's gradual transition from tribal/nomadic existence to a more settled and thus "conventionalized" modality of existence. Settled life called for a greater amount of planning and organizing on man's part, and we may speculate that this reached its peak with the great urban civilizations. In terms of human development this means that man's rational capacities, as distinct from his psychic capacity for myth, were undergoing intensified development. Planning, of course, implies the psychic ability to check and appraise one's ideas in the light of their actual effectiveness, and I have chosen to describe this new capacity as that of rationality.

From the point of view of revelation theology we can notice an increased differentiation of the signification of what we now term "revelation." In a conventionalized mode of existence, societal convention begins to replace the dominance of nature in man's consciousness. The surprising development of legal codes in the era of the great civilizations can be seen as a result of the emergence of conventional consciousness. A new "center" of existence is now required, and it is found in those conventions which stabilize and organize, and indeed serve as the very condition of possibility of, the new civilizations. In this light we can understand the "sacrality" which Israel accorded the decalogue, the ritual laws, the covenant—indeed, these were the new "centers" of existence. As this era was a transitional one, the power of rational thinking had not yet overcome the mythical. The mythical sense of "divine immediacy" and the "numinous" experience of reality were not, then, replaced but *transferred* to the new centers of conventional existence. Hence, it is "God" who reveals the decalogue and the covenant, and "revelation" begins to be restricted to these. However, as the evidence indicates, this was a very fluid period, and the new conventional "locus" of divine revelation goes hand in hand with more mythical conceptions.[5]

(3) Phase Three: The Post-Conventional (Axial) Phase of Human Consciousness

This phase, of course, is the most significant one for the Judaeo-Christian tradition, for it is only from this period that we can speak of the emergence of a Judaeo-Christian notion of revelation *in the proper sense*. It was, as we have seen, the intensification of man's rational abilities which enabled some men to cross this new threshold into axial existence. The notion of a strictly transcendent deity presupposed a highly developed rational capability: that of distancing oneself both from nature and from culture and of conceiving the possibility of what transcends both. In Israel this gave birth to radical monotheism: "I am the Lord, there is no other" (Is. 45:6). I am not, of course, maintaining that it was Israel's rational capabilities which *directly* generated the transcendent notion of God. The historical evidence indicates that the domination of Israel by foreign powers forced Israel to widen and deepen its notion of Yahweh, so that he could be seen as the Lord of all nations, and thus the one ultimately behind Israel's destiny too. As Kaufman expresses it, this led to a "vision of a single unifying activity working through the entire cosmic and historical process" which "made it possible for the first time to see all history, both cosmic and human, as a unified and meaningful whole moving forward through time toward an ultimate goal."[6] I would only maintain, however, that such a deepened notion of Yahweh presupposed man's abstractive capacities and thus witnessed to the intensified use of rationality which, we have said, characterized the axial period. Again, however, this development illustrates that man's new development in consciousness generated a correspondingly widened notion of revelation.

I am incompetent to explain the developments which occurred at this time giving rise eventually to Zoroastrianism, Buddhism, Taoism, and the reformulation of religion which occurred in Greece. My own understanding of the matter, buttressed by Jaspers, leads me to believe that a similar maturation in human consciousness made possible a new understanding of the religious quest in these other axial peoples. Further, I am inclined to think that the qualitatively new level of consciousness initiated by Jesus led to a similar reunderstanding of revelation among the early Christians. This did not, except in the case of Marcionism, lead to a denial of the Hebraic breakthrough. Rather, the early Christians' new level of understanding led them to the conclusion that what Yahweh was about had been fully manifested in Jesus. But again, the new shift of attention to Jesus—the view that he is the revelation—was possible only because of the newly expanded Christian consciousness.

(4) Phase Four: Historical Consciousness

It is the entry into historical consciousness which both "threatens" the Judaeo-Christian view of revelation and yet promises a decisive maturation in our view of it. Historical consciousness, we have said, refers to man's awareness of himself as the free and active cause behind his own development. For the proper nuances I would refer the reader back to our chapter on this subject. I only wish to point out now that it is in this phase of human development—a phase that theology is currently undergoing—that man becomes aware of the radically historically-conditioned nature of all things human. The history of theology since the Enlightenment period illustrates rather well how historical consciousness has been experienced as a threat to the Judaeo-Christian view of revelation. The reason, of course, is obvious. Man's new awareness of himself as his own free and active cause can lead in the direction of a humanism in its various manifestations. Feuerbach, in the nineteenth century, may be taken as an extreme example of this trend, in his view that revelation represents nothing more nor less than the projections of man's own mind. Historically, I have tried to show that this "reductionistic" view presupposes the overdifferentiated rational ego which characterizes our modern period.

However, and this would be my own view, this new consciousness represents a period of a possibly profound maturation for the Judaeo-Christian tradition, in which it has been forced to explore the very foundations of its faith and overcome all traces of mythical dualism, the "cultural mortgages" of previous phases of human existence. Most importantly I would maintain that an historical consciousness enables us to understand that revelation is actually a second-order concept used by man to describe what is first and foremost experienced as a development in his own consciousness itself, a development made possible by the Hebraic discovery of God and the new level of consciousness initiated by Jesus.[7] Historically, this would presuppose a more holistic view of human consciousness, in which reality is not reduced simply to the rationalistic ego, but the latter is integrated into a larger whole.

To my knowledge, the theologian who has devoted the most attention to this view of revelation made possible by historical consciousness is James Mackey.[8] Mackey stresses the importance of distinguishing the language of faith from the language of revelation. Faith-language emerges from man: "I believe . . . I acknowledge that . . . I confess." From my own perspective, this is the kind of language a man speaks when he undergoes the expansion of consciousness made possible by the Hebraic discovery of God and the resurrection belief.[9] Revelation-language, on the other hand, "speaks as from God's side": "God said. . ."; "Thou shalt not. . ."; etc. From my own perspective, this is the kind of language that Israelites and Christians spoke *after* their expansions of consciousness, after one is aware that one is dealing with God. This sort of revelation-language becomes a natural outburst of the religious mind. Mackey indicates this as well: "The very intensity of my faith conviction, my acknowledgement of a creative will in and behind the universe, revealed yet hidden by more empirical reality, cannot find adequate expression except in terms of direct speech that seems to set the speaker behind God's viewpoint, speech which is as from God's side."

What Mackey is attempting to indicate is that in ages prior to historical consciousness, and thus in ages which could not yet fully distinguish between subject and object, Judaeo-Christians generally spoke revelation-language. However, when man becomes aware of himself and his own subjective contribution to knowledge, he becomes aware that this revelation-language is a secondary one, flowing from *his own* experience of faith. This leads Mackey to the conclusion "that faith is the more fundamental concept of the two, revelation the more secondary and derivative, that faith gives rise to expectations of revelation and to revelation-talk in general and that it is not the case that revelation gives rise to faith."[10] My own conclusions lead me to a fundamental agreement with Mackey, and I

would regard the Hebraic and Christian expansions of consciousness as structurally equivalent with what Mackey intends
by "faith." In fact, we could go further and maintain that
"faith" itself is a developing reality and, in its Judaeo-Christian sense, only becomes a possibility because of the Hebraic
and Christian expansions of consciousness.

As this historically conscious view of revelation is worked
with and thought through, it lends a great deal of clarity to
many of the questions still debated by revelation-theologians.
In particular, it lends clarity to what Avery Dulles, in a recent
typological survey of revelation theories, views as the main difficulty thus far faced by theologians—namely whether "revelation is . . . an external datum that imposes itself on any sane
and honest observer" or "a free expression of one's own subjectivity."[11] The cardinal insight of the first option, which Dulles
terms "objectivist," is its refusal to reduce revelation to the
subjective fancy of the individual. In the Judaeo-Christian tradition revelation has always been interlocked with and mediated by "inspired prophets and apostles" as well as historical
events. In our developmental view, we, too, would maintain
that the Hebraic and Christian consciousness is initiated by an
"inspired vanguard," if you will, and always a function of historical events. We would regard the tradition's stress on historical events as actually an insight into the fact that revelation
was first and foremost a unique and privileged breakthrough
on the part of certain individuals into a new level of consciousness. Similarly our view both does justice to and further clarifies the cardinal insight of the second, or "personalist," option:
"Personalism has taught us that we cannot speak of revelation
without attending to the believing subject in whom revelation
initially comes to birth, and apart from whom it cannot sub-
sist."[12] Once revelation is understood *in its original form* as the
expansion of consciousness made possible by the Hebraic understanding of God and the Christian acceptance of the resurrection belief, then we can understand why "revelation" presupposes a human subject and demands one.[13] Dulles quite
rightly indicates that the personalist danger is that of isolating
"the individual in the privacy of his own experience . . . mini-
mizing the dependence of contemporary man upon past reli-

gious experience."[14] Our view, on the other hand, would stress that the Hebraic and early Christian breakthroughs are the *axis* of all true religious experience, to which all must return, and in the light of which contemporary religious experience is to be judged.

My one problem with Dulles' view, and it may be only a semantical one, has to do with his assertion that revelation is "a disciplined response that unfolds under the aegis of faith within a community and a tradition."[15] My difficulty here is with the term "response." Dulles' desire is to preserve the *objective* nature of revelation: "Revelation . . . is what enables faith to be faith."[16] My own conclusions would lead me to avoid the term "response" and to maintain, with Mackey, that "faith" *is* the "revelation," or, in our terms, revelation primordially means our expansion of consciousness. Interestingly, I think this accords with Dulles' own desires: "Revelation never exists in some chemically pure state."[17] What Dulles means, I suspect, is that the only "revelation" that exists is the one we have termed our expansion of consciousness. *The relationship is not one of "response" but of "identity."*[18]

(5) Phase Five: Transcultural Consciousness

At this stage of human and Christian development, it is difficult to assess what the possible implications of a transcultural consciousness are for revelation theologies. At the very least such a consciousness would imply, as Gabriel Moran asserts, a breakdown of the authoritarianism of Christianity and a discovery of the universal and transcultural elements in the various traditions.[19] From the Christian side it would imply that the fullness of Christianity's own promised expansion of consciousness is yet to come, and that a genuine dialogue with the world's religions may be the precise form in which this will occur. This will require, on its part, a high degree of detachment from its own "cultural" form of faith and a recognition that the crucial issue in religion is not sterile attachment to culturally limited formulations and understandings of the religious quest, but the on-going conversion made possible by wholeheartedly undergoing the expansions of consciousness which are available to all.

Thesis #3: *Since the development of human consciousness is a complexifying process, previous views of revelation, occasioned by that consciousness, are not eliminated but complexified or transformed.*

"I have come, not to abolish them [the Law and the prophets], but to fulfill them," the Scriptures say (Mt. 5:17). I would only wish to point out that from the perspective of this entire analysis, the scriptural aphorism just cited makes good sense. At this point I would only refer the reader back to our previous analyses where, at each point, it was possible to indicate how each new development in consciousness can be seen as transforming the previous levels. Because previous levels are never eradicated, it indeed becomes possible for Christians to lapse back into a pre-axial mentality, conceiving of revelation in perhaps a mythical manner, or by absolutizing their own cultural experience much as a conventional consciousness would have it. Indeed, I would maintain that the great demands that an historical and transcultural consciousness places on Christianity make the possibility of such a relapse ever more likely. But the other possibility also remains: a *transformation* of previous levels and the possible emergence of Merton's transcultural, "finally integrated" individual. Were one to seek criteria for discerning authentic revelation, I think he could do no better than to look for the signs of a fully integrated personality. Because a relapse always remains a possibility, revelation is always incomplete and eschatological.

Notes

1. Kaufman, *God the Problem, op. cit.,* pp. 148-170.
2. Avery Dulles, "The Problem of Revelation," *Proceedings of the Catholic Theological Society of America* 29 (1974) 77.
3. Kaufman, *God the Problem, op. cit.,* p. 161.
4. Richardson, *op. cit.,* p. 6.
5. Cf. Nikiprowetzky, *art. cit.*

6. Kaufman, *God the Problem, op. cit.,* p. 164.

7. Here I am prescinding from the further question of the truth or falsity of these claims.

8. Cf. Mackey, *The Problems of Religious Faith, op. cit.,* esp. pp. 190-206; and his "The Theology of Faith: A Bibliographical Survey (And More)," *art. cit.*

9. From the perspective of human consciousness "faith" itself must be said to be a developing notion. "Faith" in the proper Judaeo-Christian sense is only possible after the Hebraic entry into axial consciousness. Mircea Eliade, *The Myth of the Eternal Return, op. cit.,* p. 110, explains this somewhat: "Abraham's religious act inaugurates a new religious dimension: God reveals himself as personal, as a 'totally distinct' existence that ordains, bestows, demands, without any rational (i.e., general and foreseeable) justification, and for which all is possible. This new religious dimension renders 'faith' possible in the Judaeo-Christian sense." I am inclined to think that the axial view of faith, here expressed by Eliade, was later read back into the Abraham narratives.

10. Mackey, "The Theology of Faith: A Bibliographical Survey (And More)," *art. cit.,* 223.

11. Dulles, *art. cit.,* 98.

12. *Ibid.,* 104.

13. The truth behind Pannenberg's view that revelation can be recognized even by those who have no faith is that the revelatory experience, made possible by an appropriate expansion of consciousness, is potentially a possibility for all people. The stress is on the word "potentially." Cf. *ibid.,* 81.

14. *Ibid.,* 104-105.

15. *Ibid.,* 98.

16. *Ibid.,* 103.

17. *Ibid.*

18. This does not reduce God to human consciousness. What it does assert is that revelation has to do with the "available God," and that the available God *is* our expansion of consciousness.

19. Cf. Gabriel Moran, *Design for Religion* (New York, 1970), pp. 38-40, where he speaks of three stages in the history of the idea of revelation: pre-rational, rational, and ecumenical, roughly equivalent to our (1) pre- and conventional phases, (2) the post-conventional and historically conscious phases, and (3) the transcultural phase.

IX
God, Christ, and Human Consciousness Today

The Problem of Individuation Today: The Isolated "Ego"

The goal of our essay has been to describe and explain the emergence and development of human, but primarily Christian, *individuation*. While our thesis is hopefully an attractive one—Christian belief fosters a context in which fully individuated autonomy can develop—our times would seem to present some peculiar stresses and difficult challenges to the Christian form of individuation. While I am unable to deal with all of these difficulties, from our perspective of human consciousness perhaps the greatest one is that of the "isolated ego" which our times seem to foster. Christian individuation is, of course, in opposition to this. It maintains that the self, the ego, develops not solipsistically, but in function of its consciousness of God. The Judeao-Christian axis entered into axial consciousness because of, not in spite of, its awareness of God. Christ deepened, radicalized, and transformed this awareness of God and thereby brought into being the possibility of full individuation. John Cobb, in fact, thinks that one can meaningfully validate the Christian claim to finality precisely because of the form of consciousness initiated by Jesus. Because it is a consciousness promising full individuation, "there is no possibility of further development, only of refinement and increasing understanding of the reality already given."[1] My goal in this chapter is simply to confront the key contemporary challenge to this view from a Christian perspective.

A key factor fostering the emergence and dominance of what I am calling the "isolated ego" is the cultural shift we are presently undergoing, from a society largely characterized by stability to one that is largely unstable.[2] Through the develop-

175

ment of science and technology and the increasing complexification of life and specialization they generate, through industry and commerce and the mobility associated with them, through the accelerating tension between nations and continents, our culture has come to change rapidly, even though at an unequal pace. The communication media make us increasingly aware of the widespread diversity in values and life styles among cultures and subcultures. This cultural diversity, as we have already indicated, leads to an awareness of the vast pluralism of mind-sets among people. Unlike formerly, this pluralism appears as not merely a matter of differences about secondary matters, but touches the very presuppositions with which people approach life. Karl Rahner thus speaks of a "qualitatively new experience" of pluralism among peoples today.[3]

In a relatively stable and tightly structured culture—which was Christianity's and that of the West generally prior to the nineteenth century—it was largely possible both to know and to provide for the relatively unchanging needs of people. In the area of the churches, the unchanging spiritual needs were met by fixed methods of prayer and devotion. The unchanging pastoral needs were met by the fixed tasks involved in the *cura animarum*. The rather fixed and unchanging moral guidelines of the Church reflected the fixed and unchanging cultural atmosphere of the times. This same state of affairs held sway for the culture in general. Economically, the trades and professions did not manifest the specializations characteristic of our own times. Educationally the task of the teaching profession was to communicate the relatively fixed wisdom of mankind. Politically, the representative and thus pluralistic form of government was just emerging and still a minority form of government within the world. Our present cultural experience, however, is making new demands upon the individual. In a relatively unstable, changing, and pluralistic culture, the individual cannot simply fall back upon the culture's fixed and traditional wisdom and life-options. In this situation the individual is increasingly forced back upon himself and his own unique capacities. While our situation could summon forth the deepest kind of person, it could also lead in the direction of relativism, indifferentism, and individualism. When this occurs, as we should increasingly expect it to in our times, the danger of solipsism which characterizes the "isolated ego" becomes a real one.

A second factor which fosters our "isolated ego" is the increasing complexification of human information and the relative lack of what the ancients termed "wisdom." John Dunne has said: "It has been said that we have forgotten being, that we have turned from the pursuit of wisdom to the pursuit of science, that our age far surpasses previous ages in science, in the knowledge of particular beings, but shows no corresponding advance in wisdom."[4] One might say that ours is an informational age, vast in specialized knowledge. And it is this plethora of specialized knowledge to which all of us are exposed through our planetary media. It has been said that science has learned more, factually, about the world's structure in the last fifty years than in all the combined ages of mankind previously. However true this may be, the increasing complexification of knowledge is clearly an ambiguous reality. It does not necessarily mean that the man of today is more "educated" than his predecessors. It means that we are more exposed to the possibilities of knowledge, almost "over-exposed," and thus that we have the chance for greater depth. All too often, however, this greater availability of knowledge results in confusion, or, worse, in defense mechanisms and simplistic approaches to complex issues, or in closed ideologies. As the youth, when confronted with life's complexity, can retreat into himself and refuse the challenge of greater complexification, so today's man is easily led into an isolated retreat. For as knowledge complexifies, the need for integration is heightened, but it also becomes more difficult. The ancients, in what they called the pursuit of wisdom, felt they knew how to integrate knowledge into their lives, to be able to sift the relevant from the irrelevant, to discern the valuable from the detrimental. As Aquinas put it: "It is the wise man who orders, for the ordering of things is possible only with a knowledge of things in their mutual interrelations as well as in reference to something above and beyond them—their end."[5] But it is precisely this ability of which Aquinas speaks that is lacking or increasingly lessened today. Because integration is more difficult, it is avoided, and again the individual is locked up within himself.

Third, what moves us to the heart of the matter is the style of awareness characteristic of, and fostered by, our culture. It seems sociologically sound to say that a pluralistic, changing, information-oriented culture tends to generate a certain style of awareness and thinking. Adrian van Kaam speaks of our culture's predilection for an "introspective" mode of awareness, analysis and dissection, rather than integration and wholeness. He adds:

> Our culture sets great store by utility, efficiency, and success. It fosters aggressive analytical reflection which helps build science, technique, and efficient organization. Because we are so efficiency minded, we even examine ourselves in an aggressive analytical way when we engage in introspection.[6]

What van Kaam is pointing to is the effect upon our psyches of our self-conscious age. We can render our subjectivities transparent to ourselves through all kinds of consciousness-raising techniques, and this tends to foster an introspective narcissism locking the individual up within himself. Interestingly enough, in an age which represents man's increasing mastery over externally caused diseases—a mastery made possible by analytic thinking—more internal disorders seem increasingly predominant: ulcers, heart disease, addictions of all kinds, etc. Again, this introspective style of awareness, which breeds a kind of adult narcissism, is precisely what characterizes our isolated ego.

Erich Fromm has written:

> Psychoanalysis has given the concept of truth a new dimension. In pre-analytic thinking a person could be considered to speak the truth if he believed in what he was saying. Psychoanalysis has shown that subjective conviction is by no means a sufficient criterion of sincerity. A person can believe that he acts out of a sense of justice and

yet be motivated by cruelty. He can believe that he is motivated by love and yet be driven by a craving for maso-
chistic dependence. A person can believe that duty is his
guide though his main motivation is vanity.[7]

What he is pointing to is our complexified understanding of
ourselves, made possible by our analytic mode of awareness.
While this new understanding could definitely lead to a more
deeply integrated self, it also tends to breed a crippling self-
doubt in which the individual, precisely because he can no
longer trust his own inner motivations, is led to a preoccupa-
tion with the self, in which authentic alterity is blocked.

The application of the analytic style of thinking to the
psyche, which lies behind contemporary psychology and psychoanalysis, is complemented by a similar dissection of the
social realm.[8] One might say that since the time of Marx the
concept of social-"truth"-or-"reality" has also been given a
new dimension. Social structures are also seen to be ambiguous
and to embody ambiguous values. Economic expansion, industrial growth, and a materially high standard of living are directly related to the phenomenon of an increasingly small
wealthy elite, to ecological problems of the greatest magnitude,
and to the nurturing of egocentric, competitive and aggressive
values.[9] The individual increasingly distrusts the social fabric
and is led in the direction of a self-preoccupation.

I have decided to term the kind of self increasingly fostered by our times the "isolated ego." Admittedly this is a kind
of ideal type, and probably it rarely exists in its pure form.
After all, our Western culture is in part a product of Christianity, and the Christian consciousness stands in great opposition to this notion of the self. But oftentimes this only further
increases the problem. For today's individual often feels himself pulled in two different directions, the one stemming from
his own Christian heritage, and the other stemming from the
tendencies toward self-doubt and self-preoccupation. This inner
schizophrenia only heightens the tendency toward our isolated
ego. In part, at least, today's Christian needs a theoretical
framework which might contribute toward that integration and
unification which our times greatly call for, and thus I think

my ideal type is a justified one.

Freud is reported to have once written: "Wo Es war soll Ich werden" (Where the "Id" was should the "Ego" be)—the "Id," of course, referring to the many impulsive passions which the "Ego" must bring under control. Should this balancing of the many internal and external factors upon us not occur, the "ego" will lose itself and not achieve that sense of integrated identity which is the characteristic of mental health. It is precisely this view of the "ego" which our times are generating. Surprisingly enough it fosters the "isolated ego," for its emphasis is upon the self, upon the self's need to master and control itself. The great enemy is the loss of self.

A masterful description of our "isolated ego" has recently been provided us by Adrian van Kamm.[10] Speaking of our isolated ego's tendency toward introspection, he suggests:

> Introspective reflection tends to be analytical and aggressive. . . . It purposely loses sight of the totality and goes at its object aggressively. . . . Introspective reflection makes our own self and its urgency for instant self-realization central, embroiling us in a futile battle against time and against real or imagined competitors for success and survival. . . . *Isolated self-actualization becomes the measure of all things.*[11]

The effects of an overemphasis upon this mode of awareness are subtle and manifold. Van Kaam, in his own attempt to wrestle with this phenomenon, has discovered four key effects. First, the isolated person, by focusing upon himself, tends to be overcome by the various limitations of his own existence. "I have come to the conclusion that the person who sees himself in isolation must necessarily see himself as a depressing collection of countless limitations . . . in appearance, health, background, knowledge, temperament, virtue, intelligence, emotional range and intensity, chances and opportunities."[12] Second, this self-focusing, by locking the individual up within himself, causes the person to overrate his childhood history. "Introspection implies retrospection within his closed off inner world."[13] One becomes past-oriented and unable to envision a brighter future. Third, it leads to a crippling self-doubt and thus to a tendency to excuse one's lack of self-control. The very goal of the ego in this conception—self-mastery—is frustrated by itself. Finally, the individual increasingly loses contact with reality as it is and begins to dwell in a happier and richer fantasy life. "This fantasy world of the introspectionist is often marked by illusionary projects and make-believe accomplishments."[14]

I have spent some time upon this notion of the isolated "ego" because in its ideal-typical form, it seems to illustrate a basic tendency of human individuation since the axial period itself. You recall that the basic discovery of the axial period was that of individuality, the ability to differentiate oneself from one's immediacy and cultural environment and thus to sense that one is an autonomous "I." Now this new-found awareness of oneself as an "I" can be variously greeted. In the Judaeo-Christian axis it primarily led to a new autonomy, responsibility, and freedom, a new awareness of history as open to a future, and eventually to that historical self-consciousness which characterizes many people today.

On the other hand, the new awareness of one's individuality can lead to a heightened sense of aloneness, alienation, being different, cut off from the formerly pleasant and undifferentiated world of mythical man. My own understanding of the matter leads me to believe that this is what primarily occurred in the Oriental axis. The heightened awareness of aloneness was, we must suspect, common to all the axial forerunners. There are few better descriptions of this than those provided by the prophets of Israel. "Woe is me, I am doomed" (Is. 6:5), cries Isaiah when he becomes aware of the burden of his own individuality. And Jeremiah too knows the pain of aloneness: "Would that I had in the desert a travelers' lodge! That I might leave my people and depart from them" (Jer. 9:1). Yet because prophetic individuality was discovered in function of God, this sense of alienation was never radicalized. As Isaiah put it: "Yet my eyes have seen the King, the Lord of hosts" (Is. 6:5). In the Oriental axis, however, the sense of alienation did reach a radical form. One of the key factors contributing to this, in addition to the axial breakthrough to individuality, was the ancient notion of transmigration. In this view, of course, in its most ancient meaning, life was simply transitional, to be repeated in another form. And as Cobb puts it, "This conviction of immortality, far from comforting and reassuring the suffering individual, indicated to him that even in death he could not escape the burden and terror of existence."[15] Thus the problem of alienation was a key one for the Orient, and the new axial sense of individuality only further heightened this problem. I suspect that it is this radicalized sense of inner alienation which led the Oriental axis in the direction it took.[16]

Now a similar heightened sense of alienation—without the safeguards of the Oriental religious experience—increasingly characterizes the Western axis too, thus leading it in the direction of our isolated ego. What ultimately lies behind this is our historical self-consciousness, which heightens the awareness of the self and, given the particular conditions of our own times, radicalizes the sense of isolation. One could greet this heightened sense of alienated individuation by a relapse to a pre-axial, pre-individuated phase of existence. One could then return to the undifferentiated world of the child and deal with individuation by avoiding its challenge. Given van Kaam's own findings, this is a real possibility today. In the religious sphere especially this is a real possibility, given the fact that many are attracted to religion because it seems to provide the security that they sense they lack. However, the possibility remains of refusing to relapse, and, given the development of Western man, this seems the more likely. This refusal to escape the problem of individuation, then, intensifies the inner conflict and self-doubt, and this seems to be the situation of many today. Since the Renaissance and Enlightenment, with its self-consciousness and heightened sense of human autonomy, this has increasingly seemed the only viable position. This leads Cobb to speak of "autonomous reason" as the one contemporary challenge to Christianity.[17] I would consider this to be one form of the challenge. More fully I would say that the challenge comes from an isolated view of the self, in which individuation is seen as primarily an individualistic project of self-mastery and self-fulfillment—that is, our overdifferentiated ego that we essayed in an earlier chapter.

Christian Individuation

The goal of this chapter has been to query what form of human individuation the Christian faith promises, and what further developments it is capable of undergoing. As we have seen, the Christian claim stands in opposition to the solipsistic and isolated view of the self advanced above. Individuation, for Christianity, becomes possible in direct proportion to, not in inverse proportion to, one's awareness of God and affirmation of the resurrection belief. St. Paul's formulation perhaps remains the classic one: "The life I live now is not my own; Christ is living in me" (Gal. 2:20). Here we have the Christian affirmation that human life becomes a genuine possibility with God. But it is the axial and thus individuated meaning of human life: "I still live my human life, but it is a life of faith in the Son of God, who loved me and gave himself for me" (Gal. 2:20). In this Christian notion of individuation, the ego or self is not annulled, but co-exists simultaneously with and comes to fulfillment because of the personalized presence of God. This Christian self is not then an isolated one. St. Paul has this in mind:

> You did not receive a spirit of slavery leading you back into fear, but a spirit of adoption through which we cry out "Abba!" (that is, "Father"). *The Spirit himself gives witness with our spirit that we are children of God* (Rom. 8:15-16).

The awareness of a personalized God makes possible a personalized understanding of human existence. The awareness of a divine presence and divine initiative promotes and demands responsible personhood, and, as transformed in Jesus, enables the person to meet and confront every threat to responsibility, even death. This is why Cobb comes to what I take to be his fundamental insight into the Christian notion of the self:

> The decisive point is that the personal God was known as inwardly present without loss of responsible personhood. Indeed, God was known as inwardly present in such a way as to enhance and accentuate the sense of personhood.[18]

In addition to our historical-developmental view of how this notion of individuated personhood did, *in fact,* emerge, there exist contemporary analogous notions which can shed some light on our inquiry. I have personally found Teilhard's notion—that "in the realm of personality, union differentiates," rather than annihilates[19]—quite helpful. Just as deep interpersonal relationships enhance and develop one's own self, thus bringing about a more developed and differentiated self, so the emergence of Christian individuation precisely through a personalized awareness of God was an analogous process of differentiation—only in the latter case the awareness of the divine initiative removed the threat of any limitation to this differentiation. Similarly, psychologists who have increasingly noted the threat to full human development which our isolated ego poses have spoken of the ego's capacity and need for intimacy. In this view, the ego's goal is not one of self-mastery and self-control, which, as we have seen, is ultimately self-defeating and breeds a crippling sense of alienation and self-doubt. Rather, the ego achieves wholeness precisely by "letting go" in the experience of intimacy. This leads to Teilhard's differentiation through union, rather than to a crippling individualism. Further, it presupposes the individualist view of the ego, for one can only "let go" when one is assured of one's sense of self-worth and autonomy. It is this kind of letting go, in which the individual discovers himself by being able to go beyond himself, that the Christian notion of individuation fosters—only in the Christian case it is a radical letting go, a radical alterity, for what assures one's self-worth is not simply another limited human, but the personalized presence of God himself.

Again it is van Kaam who through his years of counseling has discovered that this Christian experience of individuation fosters a mode of awareness fundamentally different from the introspectionism of the isolated ego. In his words:

[It] is called transcendent because it enables us to transcend, that is, to go beyond, the practical and sentimental meanings things may have for us in terms of our own private needs, ambitions, drives, and expectations. Transcendent self-presence pushes us beyond the limited here-and-now meanings of our own particular problems, child-hood traumas, sensitivities, faults, and projects. In and beyond all of these, it integrates our lives contextually, that is, it helps us live in the context of the whole of reality, of which we are part, and with its divine all-pervading source.[20]

In other words, it leads us away from narcissism to radical alterity. It fosters unification and integration, not isolationism and dissection. It enables the individual to see himself *as a totality* precisely through concentrating on one's self as ultimately related to God. It looks at man, not as separated from, but as united with, an ultimate source of meaning. Thus it enables the individual to perspectivize his life, to view it against the greater background of his ultimate destiny before God. When man is cut off from his deepest source of meaning and viewed in an isolated and dissected way, he has no choice but that of isolationism. This may in great part account for the meaning-related kinds of illness of our times, such as ulcers and heart disease. Surely these latter have something to do with a loss of meaning and perspective. It is only the latter which gives one a sense of his unique identity and authentic personhood. As the spiritual tradition would have it, this is the *consolación sin causa*[21]—that self-authenticating source of personhood which frees the individual for responsible personhood.

From this perspective, then, we can return to Cobb's claim, cited earlier, that the Christian notion of individuation justifies the Christian claim to finality. If the Christian consciousness does promise a radical fulfillment of the human quest, then that claim seems justified. This need not, however, lead one to the conclusion that only Christians are promised full individuation. It does, however, lead to the conclusion that what came to explicit consciousness in the Judaeo-Christian axis is the possibility of full individuation which is the one common goal of all mankind.[22]

Notes

1. Cobb, *op. cit.,* p. 144.
2. For a somewhat different analysis of these factors, cf. my "Renewed Interest in the Discernment of Spirits," *The Ecumenist* 13 (1975) 54-59, and 14 (1975) 15-16.
3. Karl Rahner, "Der Pluralismus in der Theologie und die Einheit des Bekenntnisses in der Kirche," *Schriften zur Theologie,* Vol. 9 (Zurich, 1970), pp. 12-15.
4. Dunne, *op. cit.,* p. 95.
5. Thomas Aquinas, *Summ. cont. gent.,* 2, 24. Cf. Kieran Conley, *A Theology of Wisdom: A Study in St. Thomas* (Dubuque, 1963), pp. 83-84, for translation and commentary.
6. Adrian van Kaam, *In Search of Spiritual Identity, op. cit.,* p. 175.
7. Erich Fromm, *Psychoanalysis and Religion* (New Haven, 1963), p. 77.
8. Cf. Ernest Becker, *The Structure of Evil* (New York, 1968). I greatly respect the achievements of Freud and Marx and their successors. My difficulty is not with analytic thinking *per se,* but with analysis divorced from any larger, integrative and unifying perspective.
9. To my lay mind, a balanced view seems that of Robert L. Heilbroner, *Business Civilization in Decline* (New York, 1976). Cf., for example, p. 113: "The tendency of a business civilization to substitute impersonal pecuniary values for personal nonpecuniary ones"; and p. 114: "A business civilization regards work as a means to an end, not as an end to itself. The end is profit, income, consumption, economic growth, or whatever, but the act of labor itself is regarded as nothing more than an unfortunate necessity to which we must submit to obtain this end."
10. Adrian van Kaam, "Introspection and Transcendent Self-Presence," *op. cit.,* pp. 172-196.
11. *Ibid.,* p. 174 and p. 182 (italics mine).
12. *Ibid.,* p. 185.
13. *Ibid.,* p. 186.
14. *Ibid.,* p. 191.
15. Cobb, *op. cit.,* p. 61. The origins of this notion far exceed my competence, but I suspect that it reflects a pre-axial view of the self. Perhaps when man defines himself as a subordinate part of nature, as he seems to have done in his earliest phase (pre-conventional consciousness), he tends to view human existence analogously with the cyclical and repetitive processes of nature. A developed notion of individuation breaks this biological view of the self.
16. Oriental studies are in a state of flux, and scholars are not in agreement; thus I hesitate to make too many generalizations. Cf., however, Kenneth K. Inada, "Some Basic Misconceptions of Buddhism," *International Philosophical Quarterly* 9 (1969) 101-119. My basic problem with the Oriental axis is not with what it has accomplished, but rather with the complete adequacy of their view for a holistic understanding of man. It seems that the Judaeo-Christian axis, at least in principle, can resonate with the Oriental view primarily through its mystical tradition, and yet go beyond it and include more positive notions of the self. As the

Oriental axis becomes increasingly historically self-conscious and thus critical of itself, it may be led to a new and deepened self-understanding.

17. Cobb, *op. cit.*, p. 150.

18. *Ibid.*, p. 119.

19. Cf. any of the various works of Teilhard de Chardin. Also helpful is William Johnston, "Introduction," *The Cloud of Unknowing* (New York, 1973), pp. 7-32.

20. Van Kaam, *op. cit.*, p. 176; also see pp. 108-137.

21. Cf. Karl Rahner's exegesis of this notion of Ignatius Loyola in "The Logic of Concrete Individual Knowledge in Ignatius Loyola," in *The Dynamic Element in the Church* (New York, 1964), pp. 84-170. This *consolación* is the goal of the Oriental axis too, but it must be said that the Judaeo-Christian transcendent self-awareness promises a more radical form of *consolación* than does an altered state of consciousness in and of itself.

22. David Tracy, *op. cit.,* pp. 205-206 (italics mine), proposes the helpful distinction between an "exclusivist" and an "inclusivist" Christology: "We presuppose as fact what history and common sense alike testify: that any specific religious tradition starts with some moment or occasion of special religious insight. This moment, if authentically religious, will be experienced as a limit-experience and will be expressed in a limit-language representative of that insight and that experience. If the language and the experience bear universal implications, if they are not purely at the mercy of psychological or sociological forces which adequately explain their meaning without remainder, then we may describe this religious tradition as a universal, a major religion. Such a designation of universality implies two characteristics: the religion arises from a special historical occasion of religious insight, *but the special religious experience and language are sufficiently evocative of our common experience to bear the claim of universal meaningfulness.* . . . For this second Christocentric position, probably best described as an 'inclusivist' Christology, the disclosure manifested by the Christian proclamation of Jesus Christ is genuinely disclosive of all reality, is meaningful for our common existence, and is central for a human understanding of the limit-possibilities of human existence."

Index